Death of the Company

The Best Exit Interview That Was Never Had

J. D. ALLEN

GOLDEN ARROW PUBLISHING

DEATH OF THE COMPANY

The Best Exit Interview That Was Never Had

Copyright © 2018 by J. D. Allen

All rights reserved. No part of this book may be reproduced or transmitted in any form or by any means, electronic or mechanical, including photocopying, recording or by any information of the publisher, except where permitted by law. If you would like to use material from this book, prior written permission must first be obtained. Requests to the publisher for permission should be addressed by emailing info@goldenarrowpublishing.com.

This book should not be used as a substitute for the advice of competent, legal counsel from an attorney admitted or authorized to practice in your jurisdiction. You should never delay seeking legal advice, disregard legal advice, or commence or discontinue any legal action because of information in this book.

Cover and interior artwork by Jaime Del Villar

Layout & interior design by Golden Arrow Publishing

Published by Golden Arrow Publishing, California

www.GoldenArrowPublishing.com

ISBN 13: 978-1984190796

ISBN 10: 1984190792

SECOND EDITION

To the joy in my life that never fades.

Contents

NOTE FROM THE AUTHOR	9
INTRODUCTION	13
CHAPTER 1 - HIGHLY ENGAGED *(SELF-ACTUALIZATION)*	**23**
THE WELCOME WAGON	27
WHAT DO YOU DO?	31
LOVE NEW IDEAS	37
CHAPTER 2 - ENGAGED *(ESTEEM)*	**45**
EVERYTHING IS FUNNY	49
HR	53
THE ABYSS	56
GROOMING TATTLETALES	60
CHAPTER 3 - ALMOST ENGAGED *(SOCIAL)*	**67**
SHOOT THE MESSENGER	70
PENNY PINCHERS	77
HITLER'S REIGN	81
VERBAL VOMIT	86
CHAPTER 4 - NOT ENGAGED *(SAFETY)*	**97**
FOREVER TRAINING	100
FAREWELL FRIEND	107
BIRTHDAY WISHES	110
CHAPTER 5 - DISENGAGED *(PHYSIOLOGICAL)*	**119**
SELF-PRESERVATION	123
LIAR, LIAR	126

HAPPY FRIDAY THE 13TH	132
DETHRONED	136

CHAPTER 6 - SECRETS TO SURVIVAL — 143

CAN BULLSHIT SURVIVE?	146
JERK ALERT	151
TIPS FOR SURVIVAL	157
AVOID HELLISH LEADERS	167
EPILOGUE	181

Note From the Author

When I think back to my elementary school days, I recall seeing a poster on the classroom wall of a young gymnast doing a routine on the balance beam. I loved this picture. This athlete was strong, determined, tenacious, elegant. She was me. Or, at least an image of who I could be. The only thing I didn't care for were the words written at the bottom, "Only you can make your dreams come true." It had a nice tone of inspiration, very Disney. However, I couldn't help but disagree. Sure, it was her choice to step up and become an Olympic gymnast, but she certainly did not get there on her own.

Unintentionally, this poster grounded my beliefs about the true value and worth of group contributions. There's no way this athlete walked into a gym one day and was left on her own to become a gold medalist. She had parents, coaches, friends, teachers and medical professionals all helping to push her forward towards a bigger goal.

Decades later, I still hold on to this monumental truth as I function in the working world. The success of an entity goes beyond the work of its owner(s). It's the result of the combined efforts of all the people working within. They must rely on a team to advance their cause. Because of this, there is no question about the crucial role other people around us play when it comes to our career goals. That's why we hear phrases like, "It's not about *what* you know but *who* you know." Knowledge is powerful indeed, but what good is it if no one will help you share it by pushing your ideas forward?

As a marketing consultant, I've worked with many businesses in all types of industries—the oil and gas industry, the wedding industry, health and physical fitness, fashion retail, etc. As different as they may be, what they all have in common is the source of both their rise and their fall. *Death of the Company* focuses on the latter and describes one of the most common methods to destroying a business. It highlights the consequences of ignoring the most important business variable of all—the individual employees.

Think about all your past and present employment experiences and see if you can identify the worst one. Is there a job you hated the most? It may be the one that makes you shudder inside; the one you can blame for your bad habit of teeth grinding. Do you ever have destructive thoughts about your boss? Ever caught yourself daydreaming of accidentally dumping laxatives into her coffee or stapling his suit jacket to his desk chair? What *is* the proper way to slash someone's car tires? If you've had any or all of these thoughts, welcome to the part of life I like to call reality. You now have to admit you're human just like the rest of us.

I thought this book would be a quick write. Unfortunately, every time I sat down to hash out a section or two, the whole topic of ignoring employee needs quickly drained my enthusiasm. I was creating my own Catch-22. I wanted to illustrate how team members lose motivation for their work but was losing my own energy just thinking about it. It turns out *The Office* experience is only funny when you're an impartial observer, not when you're actually a part of the chaos. Thankfully, I was able to push forward in the hope that this true story could help leaders optimize their human resources (literally) by shedding light on human relations and personal needs in the workplace. There's also several tips provided to help those following a leader to survive the mishaps that may occur along the way.

Whether you're a business owner delegating from afar, a president only seen as the face of the company, a manager controlling daily operations or a team leader temporarily working with a small task force, it's important to remember that the people taking your direction are so much more than a mere tool. They are the energy that generates success in a multidimensional way. They consume your vision and represent you to everyone they come into contact with, including your target customer base. Valuing these people for their skillsets is crucial to achieving the goals of any organization. Their personal success and the success of their business are not mutually exclusive. They are directly linked and depend on one another to progress forward.

Remember: These people aren't just employees, they are teammates. They shouldn't be working *for* you but *with* you. And, you're more than a boss. You're a leader.

———————— DEATH OF THE COMPANY ————————

Note: The names within this true story have been changed to protect the (non)innocent. According to the local exorcist, evil is only dispelled when confronted openly. However, my lawyer trumps the exorcist and I am forced to change the names.

Introduction

Let's take a look at your personal weather forecast. If it's sunny outside, your feelings of happiness will shine through and you'll be motivated to engage with life around you. When the temperature drops and the weather begins turning gray, you instinctively head for shelter just like all those people you were previously engaged with. The safety of a roof over your head and the warmth of a fireplace bring a satisfying level of comfort and peace. There's no need to stand out in the rain when a dry place is easily accessible.

At work, our minds have the same response. But now, the daily forecast is indicative of the office culture established by your routine interactions with colleagues. When the sun is shining through your office window, goals are being met and you're getting paid well, it puts you in a positive state of mind and you're more interactive on all levels. Your coworkers are not only good people, you probably consider several of them friends, often enjoying each other's company outside the office. In this uplifting environment, smiling faces can be found in more places than just by the water cooler.

Now pull out your umbrella because when your boss gets angry, profits are low and your manager is about to rain havoc on your desk, it's natural to reach for your life preserver of sick days in order to wait out the storm. Threatening pay cuts and downsizing aren't the only things putting everyone in a bad mood. The interaction between colleagues begins dwindling to just a few words here and there, preferring only to bond over your mutual hatred of hovering superiors. As for the company barbeque coming up, you RSVP: Not in this lifetime! You'd rather get sucker-kicked by a kangaroo then spend more of your time surrounded by stressful people.

These forecast fluctuations are just as inevitable as the business cycle or the four seasons of a year. A business will have its high seasons and its low seasons; it will face times of expansion and recession. No business is exempt, including the one you own and/or go to work for every day. But, no matter what comes our way as the seasons change, it's not what happens to us that defines who we are, but how we *respond* to what happens to us. Just the same, it's how we respond to these economic and industry fluctuations that will ultimately define the level of employee engagement, internal support and general stability of our work life.

For the sake of structure, this truly heinous, personal story is organized using Abraham Maslow's *Hierarchy of Needs*. As a world-renowned expert on human behavior, this well-respected psychologist developed a pyramid to help illustrate his theory of human motivation and its direct connection to our personal needs in everyday life. Imagine a personalized thermometer where the red line goes up when our needs are met and down when they're ignored. It's the same with the needs pyramid. We move up and increase our engagement levels when our needs are met and back down when they're not.

Maslow then retrofitted the pyramid to specifically identify the needs of people in the workforce and how it correlates with their level of engagement that could potentially determine levels of productivity. Maslow provided a clever perspective when dissecting this deceivingly complex, yet basic question, "What motivates people?" and broke it down for us to understand. He wowed his audiences with how easy it was to see why some employees never perform to their fullest potential. Why do some people hate their jobs while others love it? What do people need in order to perform to the best of their abilities? What needs are being ignored? Who is ignoring them?

The *Hierarchy of Needs* is typically explained from bottom to top, where lower level needs must first be satisfied before an individual can move upward and achieve happiness through hierarchical advancement. I don't necessarily mean physically moving up in a company through promotions but rather moving up the pyramid as your personal needs are met. Skipping a step is, unfortunately, not an option. When I begin playing a new game, for instance, I can't expect to immediately advance to level five without first completing one through four because the skills and tools earned in those beginning levels are needed to move forward.

Why is reaching the top of the pyramid so important? Because this is where your fullest potential is waiting for you! It's the peak of unhindered progress. It's the point in your life when you have no more basic, distracting concerns about where your next meal is going to come from or where you're going to sleep; it's when you're at ease because you're surrounded by like-minded individuals who wish to move forward and grow as you do. You recognize your own value and are given the freedom to contribute to something you truly care about in a challenging and rewarding environment.

Abraham H. Maslow – Hierarchy of Needs

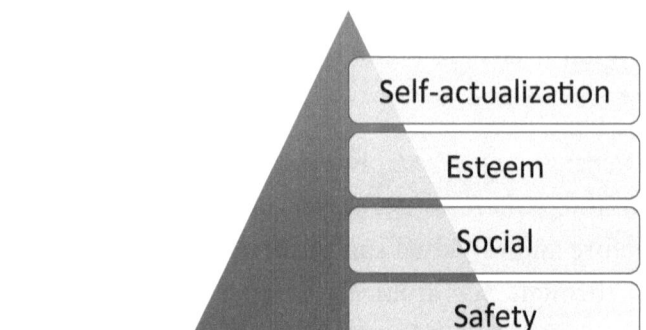

Here is a brief summary of the five levels within Maslow's *Hierarchy of Needs*:

1. *Physiological* Needs – Our basic needs require more immediate, daily attention to ensure survival than do the stages above because it involves the

maintenance of our bodies—breathing, eating food, drinking water, sleeping and staying warm.
2. *Safety* Needs – These needs establish a sense of security in having plentiful resources for maintaining our health, constant employment and even owning personal property. This may include but is not limited to having grocery stores nearby, a steady job to support yourself and a functional vehicle to go to and from all these places. When these needs are met, our mind is free to move up the pyramid and concentrate less on our physical state and more on our mental wellness.
3. *Social* Needs – Our psychological needs begin here where we desire personal connections through friendships, family interactions and sexual intimacy. This sense of belonging can be achieved when we engage with others around us.
4. *Esteem* Needs – This stage focuses on how important we feel with our individual and group responsibilities. The respect of others leads us to develop a positive sense of self, confidence and embrace personal achievements.
5. *Self-actualization* Needs – The top of the pyramid is where we are better equipped to truly achieve self-fulfilling, intellectual needs of morality, creativity, spontaneity, problem solving and the acceptance of reality. We have more mental clarity in this level than in any other because we can understand issues that were not a priority in the stages below. Our skills become amplified by the supportive

encouragement of key, influential people in our lives that may include family members, work superiors and religious leadership. They understand who we are, how we function and what we need to embrace our potential.

Leaders can guarantee a high level of synergy and success within a working environment by helping their individual team members tap into this energy source. Doing this is a win/win for everyone involved! Why would a leader make the conscious choice to work with someone who is at the lower end of the pyramid, utilizing only a small portion of their potential due to basic worries, when that exact same employee could be substantially more productive? Just the same, how can an individual comfortably unleash the full realm of their creativity within *Self-actualization* when they don't have the *Social* support and acceptance from their colleagues? True leaders will proactively assess the struggles of their team and provide the necessary support needed both individually and collectively. This concept is the cornerstone of a leader's purpose.

Purposes of This Book

To add a little entertainment value, *Death of the Company* will explain Maslow's *Hierarchy of Needs* in reverse beginning at the top where highly engaged enthusiasm can be found and proceed down the destructive path of ignoring employee needs. Assuming everyone has the capabilities to achieve *Self-actualization*, let's start with the positive feelings that come with an unhindered sense of accomplishment and success. The main purpose of moving backwards or down the pyramid is to further highlight how an entity, even with all the necessary (human) resources, can manage to self-destruct by not paying attention to its most valuable resource—the individuals that make up the team.

According to psychological research, only a small percentage of people ever make it to the top of Maslow's hierarchy. The reason for not attaining *Self-actualization* varies depending on several factors. With that said, I believe everyone has the ability to reach a true state of happiness in the workplace if they choose to and *Death of the Company* wishes to focus on a specific type of leader who is solely responsible for destroying their business by pushing individuals back down the pyramid rather than encouraging their journey upward.

All growth within each stage is directly correlated to general happiness, personal satisfaction and quality of self-image. Everyone must first satisfy their needs within the stages below in order to advance to the stages above. For instance, you probably don't feel secure in your position at work if you're barely surviving on minimum wage. You may not feel you belong in an environment where others are always promoted above you. You wouldn't feel important when your boss fails to keep you busy and engaged with work tasks that are aligned with your capabilities. You also wouldn't enjoy the blissful feelings of being on the top of the world when you don't feel important and needed in a safe and secure workplace.

At the beginning of each chapter you'll find one of Maslow's five stages explained further and how it pertains to an individual's motivation and personal involvement at work. I'll also identify the key areas where leadership has mismanaged by slipping on their own banana peel. But, I'll leave it to you, the reader, to decipher where and/or how many times the errors are made. You may even pinpoint several other flaws you can personally identify with. If you've ever experienced undue pressure and stress at work, I predict you'll find a few. If you've ever been forced to work under incompetent management, I predict you'll find several (hundred) more.

No need to worry. You don't need a business degree to appreciate the mini-stories held within these pages. Everyone has felt or witnessed the isolation of a disgruntled supervisor, the rejection of a once friendly peer, or the disrespect from an egotistical boss. And, if by chance, you haven't come into contact with any of these issues, the better equipped you'll be after reading for when they do happen.

Chapter

1

HIGHLY ENGAGED

Self-actualization

Welcome to Happy-Land! Inspiration Point!

At the top of every peak is the most notable and coveted position, or in this case, mental ideation of everyone who spends part of their day in a work setting. The top signifies both importance and rarity. *Self-actualization* is the most difficult to achieve because, like any mountain, you must first climb the lower levels before the psyche begins acknowledging true satisfaction from the journey below.

This viewpoint allows for a better perspective of our surroundings. Those individuals who have reached it are easy to spot because they're few in number and are more distinguished amongst their colleagues with their high-quality work ethics and positive sense of self. They're hardworking, genuinely happy and have the rest of us asking, "How do they do it?"

Within *Self-actualization*, a person has a healthy understanding of their potential and ability to grow. Truth, wisdom, and justice are the crown jewels found on this mountaintop. A person at the top has the ability to comprehend and sympathize with the feelings and needs of others. They don't fear the talents and abilities of those around them but openly acknowledge and assign tasks accordingly. Because the majority of their personal needs are met, their focus can be redirected towards helping their colleagues meet their own needs.

Additional characteristics of the *Self-actualized* include having a good sense of humor and uplifting the people around them. They are outwardly focused on others and group problems rather than inwardly on themselves alone. They are able to view scenarios objectively, entertain opposing thoughts coming from multiple directions and are more receptive to a democratic environment of group contributions. They are often resistant to extreme enculturation by encouraging creative, innovative thoughts and affirmative actions. Although these leaders find great satisfaction in maintaining interpersonal relationships with a few key people, they also hold great importance on privacy where they can reflect on the ethical standards and repercussions of their work-related decisions.

For some people, reaching the top of this pyramid will be one of the most strenuous hikes of their lives. Those individuals who can look within themselves and are honest about who they are, what they want, and most importantly, what they need, will have an easier time and a clear advantage over those who prefer a blind approach. This is not one of those moments when ignorance is blissful. In essence, self-reflection is the best way to *Self-actualization*.

Ask yourself questions about the real motivations behind your career goals and answer them honestly. What matters most to your cubicle cellmate may not be as important to you. You may realize that making money is not as significant to you as opportunities to learn. Perhaps your boss puts the need for affiliation much lower on his priority list while you, on the other hand, would hate a workday with no one to talk with. Priorities differ amongst individuals and so will the answers to these questions.

It's important to understand that *Self-actualization* is a continual state of learning and growth rather than an end point of utopian existence. As time changes, so too do our desires and needs change. What your surrounding community looks like now is probably nothing compared to what it was a few daces ago. What you expected out of life as a teenager was no doubt vastly different than what your expectations are now. So, it makes sense that our personal goals and future plans can also be adjusted to a new set of values as time continues to bring new adventures our way.

It's also important to note that the pyramid does not necessarily measure success. The chart illustrates how our motivation to put forth additional effort increases as our personal needs are met. Although, where you stand on the chart is a good indication of your potential to succeed. You're not going to get promoted to an executive position while gasping for breath at the bottom of survival mode and being at the top doesn't necessarily mean zero struggles or management conflicts. However, those situations can become easier to cope with when you're within *Self-actualization.*

Now back to that projected forecast when you're sitting at the top of the pyramid.

Company Culture Weather Forecast: Sunny with clear skies and positive thinking.

The Welcome Wagon
Embracing Toxicity

My personal career ambitions directly out of college included focusing on a startup that was guaranteed to pay off my student loans and ensure future stability. Positions I held in the past taught me how to delegate which was a proud achievement considering it's one of the most common downfalls of those in leadership positions. I had tapped into my network of friends with backgrounds in all areas of small business including legal, web and graphic design, logistics, etc. I was putting in a solid 50% of my energy into this project. So, naturally, it was coming along slower than a work meeting from hell.

Wishing to take advantage of my idle state, a friend of mine, Dr. Victoria Carter, asked if I would be willing to spend a few hours assisting her at a business she was recently hired to restructure. She was being polite of course. She knew I could use the money and gain some more experience should I get wind of the concept that working for someone else may help pay off my debt more quickly than starting something from scratch.

Victoria also knew this was the kind of setting I could thrive in. It was a nonprofit business designed to provide a long list of personal services and resources to clients such as personal counseling, substance abuse interventions and legal consultations. There were also information resources available similar to dialing 2-1-1 where representatives connect community members with public agencies that assist with housing needs, childcare, healthcare and much more. It was a fantastic resource that I would soon begin calling "Life's Cheat Sheet for Adults."

I quickly became privy to the unpublicized reason Dr. Carter had originally been hired—to increase the company's credibility. Apparently, the business was under scrutiny for failure to retain a clinical psychological on staff who would help direct efforts and upgrade quality control. Hiring Victoria was vital to the company's stability and delighted the president so much that he'd yell, "Victoria is ours!" every time she would walk by.

To complicate matters further, the business itself possessed a toxic working environment internally. It was a war zone littered with strategic bombs in the form of backstabbing, tattle-tailing and conspiracy theories. Attention was desperately needed in-house. The combination of Victoria's doctorate and our individual experience with improving work environments ensured things would progress in the right direction. Focused and ready, we wasted no time in moving forward.

What's one of the first steps in improving a toxic work environment? Remove the threat of toxicity. Before I arrived around 9 a.m. on my first day, two people had been let go just an hour prior. The tension in the air was thick but I was prepared for that. No doubt, everyone was on the defense, unsure of what security still existed within the company. None-the-less, everyone greeted me kindly, including the two owners who behaved slightly more ecstatic at my arrival than the rest. That wasn't too surprising. After all, they weren't out of the loop. They knew exactly what was going on. Their security was fully established because they weren't in danger of losing their jobs.

My welcome hour included a description of my duties and the part-time hours I would accept. Not expecting to stay for more than a few months, I accepted the $13.50/hour pay but announced the importance of being able to rearrange my schedule at will because of my own business activities I had a primary responsibility to. The owners had no problem with this arrangement and were even pleased to hear how my marketing background could contribute to their success. Everyone was happy, so I signed on the dotted line as "Marketing & Program Coordinator."

I started learning the ropes by answering calls alongside a guy named Oscar as his relief and providing services per client request. Before I arrived, he was the youngest employee on staff, somewhere in his late 20's. He had been in the same position for years and had the responsibility of training over a dozen people, including several managers hired for positions above him. Oddly enough, Oscar himself had never been promoted to any of these management positions. I would wait to probe on that topic another time.

My day or two of training and interacting with Oscar suggested that he was more than capable of performing almost every job in the entire office perfectly. I enjoyed his calm, introverted nature that welcomed any question I had. And, despite all the tension in the air, it didn't take long for the rest of the office staff to accept me as one of their own, too.

Getting to know everyone one by one, I began to value their daily conduct on both a personal and professional level. In return, they began appreciating my abilities to work alongside as their relief. I made it clear that I was their aid, not their equal, and I could continue learning from their experience. Most of them were understandably reserved until they had a chance to size me up and compare me to those who were just fired. I was a new chess piece on the board and they needed to figure out what role I would play amongst them. Only then would they open up and begin revealing what kind of nightmare I had truly got myself into.

So, let the unraveling begin.

What Do You Do?
Your Job

Mr. Chief Executive Officer (CEO), Herbert, publicly complained that his wife and Chief Financial Officer (CFO) and co-owner, Karen, had to work constantly on the weekends. Not enough was accomplished at the office and she'd spend her free time doing more than just crossing her "T's" and dotting her "I's." He glared down at the employees who were in the middle of taking phone calls. It didn't take a genius to figure out where he placed all the blame. Although, I was a little surprised how noisy he was about it. Perhaps, he was just having a bad day and this type of passive aggressive management style wasn't his preferred method of communication.

In an effort to relieve stress, Dr. Carter offered to take on more responsibility and suggested Karen teach her how to produce monthly utilization reports. This document was given to all of our client companies to outline the services provided to their employees on a monthly basis. Dr. Carter was a capable researcher who could easily keep track of how many calls were coming through, how many appointments were had and several other variables that would require the development of charts and graphs. Maintaining a list of tally marks wouldn't be a problem.

Karen's response to Dr. Carter's suggestion was interesting to say the least. For a lack of better words, she freaked out. "Absolutely not!" was her only response and became alarmingly twitchy as she stormed off to her office. Dr. Carter had identified a need she could fulfill but was forced into silence by the very person who needed the help. It was odd that Karen would reject her when, at that very moment, I was watching Oscar create the final utilization documents on his computer. A bottom-level employee could do it but a doctorate-level manager was not allowed to? What exactly was going on here? More importantly, why was everyone in the office pretending like our boss had not just thrown a public temper tantrum?

Staffing 101

Karen wasn't the only one aggravated most parts of each day, so was everyone else. The only uplifting behaviors shined through when we interacted by telling stories and tossing paper-made toys on to one another's desk in between phone calls. To Herb's credit, it did seem that my new coworkers struggled to perform basic job responsibilities. They were obviously intelligent people, but I could sense their spirits were low. It almost seemed like they didn't enjoy their jobs. How unfortunate, because I was enjoying the task of helping others immensely with one notable exception—I wasn't being assigned any marketing tasks.

To my horror, I realized that more than half of the people in the room felt the same as I did. Optimal performance would never be attained because every single person was doing someone else's job. No one had been given tasks that matched their abilities or interests. It was like watching a child trying to shove a square peg into a round hole before it finally breaks and some of the pieces go through. In their infinite wisdom, the owners determined that the secretary would perform billing tasks, the accountant would organize events, and the individuals with marketing and graphic design backgrounds were on the front lines answering phone calls. With a little departmental rearranging, we could automatically upgrade performance levels! I hoped more than believed that the owner's inability to observe individual expertise was more of an oversight than a character flaw.

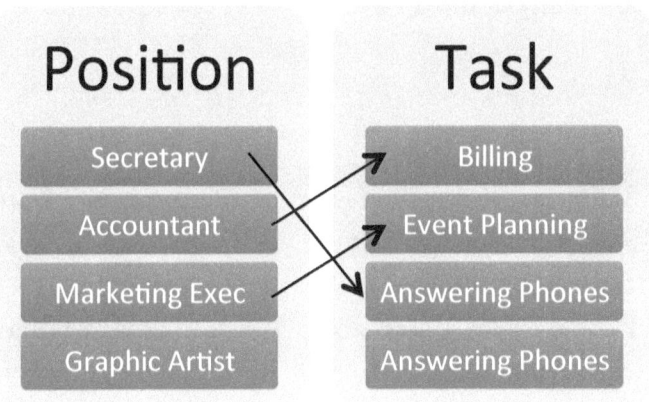

Even if a manager successfully hires quality workers, they unknowingly settle for a B-level team when they could easily have those exact same employees perform at an A+ productivity level by takin the time to identify employee abilities based on education, past experience and ability to learn. Otherwise, these people get assigned tasks not congruent with or proportional to their strengths which means daily tasks are continually performed with subpar enthusiasm at best. My coworkers weren't incapable. They were unhappy.

A very clear message had been communicated from upper management to everyone below. The slouched over, slow working demeanors surrounding me revealed that the message was received loud and clear. The personal skills of these employees were not valued as much as their physical presence which was only needed to do someone else's bidding. Rather than being viewed as an integral part of a successful team, my new friends were seen as dispensable items that only drained the company's revenue stream.

Large and in Charge

Adding to the chaos created by inappropriate staffing, the owners tried maintaining a "large and in charge" business image with less than a dozen employees. A call would come in for Karen and she would routinely have it sent to someone else. After all, she was important, busy and owners of companies were always difficult to get ahold of. More accurately, she was terrified of speaking with the public and pretending to have a large business structure was a convenient shield. It's common for small business owners to project a decentralized front to give consumers the impression of a much larger, and therefore, successful business. But, the opportunity cost is all that time wasted on faking it.

> "When complaints roll in, Karen pushes all her calls onto me. Then she stands over my shoulder mid-call, dictating every single word I'm supposed to say. Email responses are no different, either. She basically writes the whole message and then tells me to send it. I'm her human shield meant to protect her from any conflict that could potentially derail her motives."
>
> ~ Kevin

The odd part (just in case things aren't weird enough for you yet) was how the owners also tried playing this same game with their own employees. What's worse, because there was such a small number of us (the ratio of managers to general employees was roughly 1:1) and everyone could easily see one another from where they sat working, there was no confusion about when your concerns were being ignored. Karen and Herb would simply go into their offices and stop speaking to you altogether. They would then send a court jester in their place to relay some unwelcome, trivial message, "Your request for vacation has been denied," or, "We need you to rearrange your personal schedule and work different hours today." My personal favorite was always, "Did you get the time change memo? Don't want you to be late for work."

This office was 100 percent centralized. The power used for decision-making was not a shareable commodity. There was no open communication stream between the owners and the hired help. The clients were at the same disadvantage, too. As a result, the quality of communication was comparable to playing *Telephone* with chimpanzees. It just wasn't happening. Although, there were plenty of us scratching our heads.

I got a small taste of this nonsensical behavior a few days before I left the office to give a scheduled presentation for a client company. There was an indepth conversation had about what I would wear. A conversation, mind you, that I was not invited to join even though specific questions were asked regarding what types of clothing my wardrobe had to offer. "She should wear... Do you think she would... I wonder if she has more dresses. I like her in dresses." Um, hello. I'm standing right here. Why don't you just ask me?

I was beginning to get a little creeped out (for a lack of more sophisticated terms). I learned much too late that I had willingly subjected myself to a corporate culture of idiocracy where opposite-land reigned supreme and you weren't doing it right unless you were doing it wrong. No one had the opportunity to contribute to company goals because...

Wait a second. What *were* the goals of this business?

Love New Ideas
So Sad We Can't Use Them

When times of trouble find a way through a company's door (and they always do), it's often noted first by the lowest level employees, someone who is on the frontline of day-to-day operations. A competent employee first attempts to reduce the severity of an urgent problem and then reports the extent of the issue to their direct supervisor as soon as possible. That is, if anyone will listen.

The last global company I worked for gave me the marketing title and pay I wanted but wouldn't allow me to actually do anything of substantial worth. The first meeting I ever had with the CEO, I was given permission to speak candidly and wasted no time in doing so. He loved my enthusiasm to improve our website's visual appeal and ease of use, and I was encouraged to create a plan of action that would be reviewed for approval. Unfortunately, that never came to fruition despite my capabilities and eagerness. Any efforts to improve the company's accessibility and image were praised in the beginning and ignored later on. My options were to either sulk in the corner and continue personal assistant tasks or be proactive in my efforts. Unfortunately, instead of utilizing me, the CEO wasted over a year and then redid the website himself! Result? Just as confusing but with a few more fuzzy photos to look at.

Personal experiences like this provided me with more insight on how to approach employers, such as Karen and Herb, who were hesitant to delegate important tasks to others. After meeting some of our company's clientele directly, I suggested several changes to Karen that would improve the company's image and attract more clients. Understanding that finances were a sensitive issue, I started by highlighting small, basic contributions before easing her into the much-needed bigger changes. At least I tried to.

What I said: *"Our table presentation at public events is somewhat lacking and has the potential to create negative images of the company brand in the eyes of our clientele. To enhance our current methods, I would like to suggest we purchase a few low-cost items that will improve this image and cater to both current and potentially new clients."*

What I meant: *"The fact that you're satisfied hanging up a small, dirty, creased-by-a-fold company logo sign is completely horrifying and unprofessional. I'm also embarrassed to sit at a promotional table that offers year-old candy stored in our supply closet that may or may not have been recently bombed for insects with Raid. People will not stop by if there are merely pamphlets on the table. We must provide them an experience they can enjoy that will create buzz amongst their colleagues."*

Like all newbies before me, I was completely shut down. "We've purchased things before without receiving any benefit," was her only response. My second and third attempts were cut short and she looked down at her desk indicating the conversation was over. There would be no more talk of improving anything let alone spending money.

I failed. There's no other way to express that. I failed in less than two minutes.

Despite the owners being very pleased with my work ethic and capabilities, I found I held little influential power. Once again, I found myself unable to contribute. I was to do my job and no more. More accurately, I was to do what they said and no more. My role was to be an eager puppy at their heels, submissive to their every demand. The only perk available was that I got to use a human's bathroom. But, I would not despair! I'd work on increasing my level of influence by winning a few smaller battles first.

It was frightening how difficult management made things for everyone in the office, and by recourse, difficult for themselves. I had run into a few unforeseen brick walls. I wasn't hurt (thanks, I know you were concerned), but I began to see why none of my colleagues made an effort to improve current standards and why everyone seemed to be giving me the, "Aw, isn't she cute," face. Did they know something I didn't?

Final Thoughts
Chapter 1

Think back to the last job you held? How did you learn the ropes? When did you meet your coworkers? What was the initiation period like? Socialization probably began with learning the goals of the organization and how your new position contributes. Daily tasks were assigned and proper introductions made. A clear picture of the company's culture began to appear when you witnessed firsthand how willingly your new colleagues embraced the company's rules and daily practices that lead towards group cohesion and the achievement of said goals. If this wasn't what happened, you may have left work or are still leaving work today asking yourself questions like, "What do I actually do here? What is my purpose?"

Karen and Herb's attempt to socialize their new employees happened on two levels – the owners versus everyone else. This "us vs. them" mentality is dangerous to any environment whether inside the office or out. It's comparable to having two different leaders, two different sets of priorities, two different ways of thinking. Essentially, it's two opposing paths headed in opposite directions. These clashing perspectives won't magically generate excellent company results. It's like trying to make a baby sleep during a live rock concert. It's just not going to happen.

No one was on the same page at my office. In fact, they were purposefully against each other, a distance set in place and reinforced everyday by the owners. A power struggle at its finest creates a company culture of confusion. The tension was so thick that one of the directors would leave the office every single day at lunch only to eat a homemade meal in his car and listen to books on tape. The poor guy had to go elsewhere to breath and digest his food.

Out of all the businesses I've worked with, it's the leaders who start a business, own it, and also run the day-to-day operations that are the most difficult to work with. And, I get it. The business is their baby. However, the same thing will happen to their company as it would to an actual child. If you hover over and dictate your child's every move, they'll become socially awkward, unable to play comfortably and appropriately amongst their peers after being denied the experience gained from a variety of interactive situations. The same thing happens with a business. If an owner hovers and hoards all the decision-making, they've lost. They think they've held onto their power of control but have lost their collective, team mind as a result.

In order to obtain commitment and loyalty from a new employee, the first few weeks of socialization are the most important for management to demonstrate the new hire's value within the business. The level of organization immersion is directly correlated with the company's values. Management must take care to nurture those values regularly, otherwise goals are rewritten by a different group of people, the veteran employees themselves who are focused on personal survival rather than company success.

As for a business owner being overworked, that's one of the oldest issues in the book. More often than not, it's also a self-inflicted struggle. Leaders make a daily choice to maintain control the only way they know how. Why should Karen and Herb blame themselves for failure when they've hired a dozen scapegoats? Accusing subordinates is much easier even though, to quote Thomas More (*Utopia*), they would "suffer their people to be ill-educated, and their manners to be corrupted from infancy, and then punish them for those crimes to which their first education disposed them…"

Identifying a few mistakes:

- Why are company goals not communicated?
- Why would you fail to delegate daily tasks to optimize your time?
- Why would you assume you're the only one with socialization power?
- Why do you think hiding behind your office window makes you invisible?
- Why would you think that was a one-way mirror?

BECAUSE YOU'RE NOT DOING IT RIGHT UNLESS YOU'RE DOING IT WRONG!

Chapter

2

ENGAGED

Esteem

Sure, I noticed employees drowning in a sea of unaddressed issues that would cause even the most experienced fish to raise a red flag out of concern. But nobody had actually died yet, so there was at least one positive thing to keep me going. And, God bless my innocent soul because that's all I needed. Things could definitely be improved and I knew I had the capabilities to do just that. I would not be dragged down by something so common as poor leadership.

Failing to keep any team on the same page is usually a communication problem. Sounds like an easy fix, right? However, for many leaders out there, it's anything but simple. Internally, it always seems like the separate departments of a business are always waging war against one another. You'll hear it daily in hospitals when nurses complain about the superiority of doctors or in schools where teachers often despise the priorities given to the directors of sports programs. The sales department ignores concerns at the inventory level. The shipping department ignores problems addressed by the sales team. Upper management doesn't understand the accounting struggles. The complaining goes on and on while corporate goals slowly get replaced with personal ones. This negative pattern becomes cyclical in nature and desperately begs for someone with the big picture in mind to disrupt its momentum.

Scanning around my office, I saw the exact opposite. No departments were battling for attention. They all seemed to appreciate one another's contributions and confidently sought help when needed. This free, honest flow of pertinent information was impressive. Even so, there still seemed to be something lacking. I saw everyone doing what they were told, but there was no real personal investment beyond. There was satisfaction upon completing tasks but definitely no joyful feelings during the process. I couldn't find an exchange of ideas, no blossoms of creativity, no involvement beyond the minimum requested. What was stifling all this energy?

I definitely didn't love working in this environment, so I jumped down the Needs Pyramid to begin contemplating other aspects of my job that you may relate with. Is my position important? Am I an essential part of this team? I question more than just my status but my independence and self-respect, too.

Maslow splits our Esteem stage into internal and external motivators. Internal motivation is based on the personal goals we set for ourselves such as improving the quality of service provided to customers by going the extra mile, befriending coworkers to improve group cohesion, or increasing your sales goals just for the personal satisfaction and positive self-esteem boost you get when you're successful.

External motivation is based on reward systems established from the outside. This could be a raise or promotion from your superiors, bonus incentives or even public recognition for work achievements. This positive attention and praise from others encourages individuals to be highly engaged at work because they feel important and valued. Respect and continual recognition is paramount to employees maintaining this engagement and making personal improvements on their own.

Company Culture Weather Forecast: Sunny with a light breeze pushing in scattered cumulous clouds and moderate levels of contentment.

Everything is Funny
LOL

Things were quickly heading south and all the owners could do was laugh. No, I don't mean they had a great sense of humor and found light-hearted joy within this concentration camp of lost hopes and dreams. In fact, I don't think I've seen them genuinely laugh ever unless it was at someone else's expense. When they don't know what to do or say in a social situation, their automatic response setting is laughter. They laugh during meetings to avoid saying, "That's a stupid idea." They laugh after awkwardly greeting an employee. They laugh after giving instructions, ending a phone conversation and commenting on the weather. (I thought the weather was supposed to be the safest topic of them all!)

I love a good laugh just as much as the next person, but all this nonsensical L-O-L behavior had me shouting in the middle of the office, "Did I miss a joke? What is so funny?!"

> "After proofing one of my monthly promotional fliers, Karen returns it to me insisting that I find a different image of a woman who wasn't so pretty. 'Some people find that offensive,' she said with her awkward giggle. OR, she's ugly and is sad about it."
> ~ Oscar

A description of the owners may help shed some light on the psychologically twisted realm in which I found myself. Herb, the president and CEO, was a feebly pudgy man in his mid-70's that would only catch your eye if the sun reflected off the numerous gold jewelry accessories cluttering his fingers and around his neck. He didn't seem to have any extensive, formal education. He's the type to display every possible status symbol available and a degree was never one of them. It's common knowledge that he was once an alcoholic and continues to struggle with the issue regularly. In public, he refers to himself as "Modest Herb" which causes everyone in earshot to roll their eyes and throw up in the nearest trash bin.

When he wasn't putting on a show and attempting to overdramatize his level of power, he consumed an enormous quantity of energy drinks daily. His favorite method of coping with stressful situations was to walk away mid-sentence and shut his office door behind him, leaving his wife to clean up where he just took a royal dump. He spent most of his time in the isolated safety of his office fiddling on his cell phone and occasionally typing emails with his two index fingers. When he couldn't find the "Send" keys, tech support was called in for reinforcements.

His counterpart, Karen, was a small, picturesque villain with a quick step. Like a mouse searching for cheese, so too, a bat hunts for blood. She was previously an elementary school administrator before making the transition to work with her husband. There were several rumors floating around about why she no longer worked in that industry, but as most rumors go, none of them made her look good. Her method of coping with stress involved using the word "no," even if someone was announcing that the bathrooms were out of toilet paper. Post-its were a secretarial comfort blanket and one of her main replacements for human interaction as she'd walk around the office sticking notes to everything except your forehead. She also didn't appreciate being called "ma'am" because it made her feel old which was exactly why most of the staff did so regularly.

Taking everything into account, I determined they made a fantastic couple. They both looked uncomfortably similar (to the point where I once considered incest a possibility) and had the combined technological skills of a devout Amish laborer. Karen had an uncanny resemblance to the creature, Smeagol, from *Lord of the Rings*, while Herb looked like he belonged in a caricature drawing. Their social skills may have been rudimentary at best, but their grandeur thoughts of success elevated their royalty status in a fantasy world all their own. Their individual needs for power were extremely high, and they both entertained high levels of paranoia that didn't allow for even the smallest amount of trust. Most importantly, they held a strong commitment to their farm animals at home that possessed a better healthcare plan than any of the employees working for them.

So we have an ex-alcoholic who pretends to manage a resource center while his ball-busting wife makes all the real decisions, causing him to cling to the only legal stimulus within his reach (insert Monster ad). So, in a world where *Office Space* meets *Breakfast Club*, there is one point that is abundantly clear. There's plenty to laugh at.

HR
Department of 1

Few top executives actually know what's going on at the lower levels of their company. In their defense, many of them don't realize there is a problem until someone finally has enough courage to speak up. At this office, however, you could be screaming at the top of your lungs and the owners would consciously ignore you. They'd lock themselves in a room, occasionally shooting a glance through their office window, attempting to determine what the main problems were and how to solve them, all without once speaking to the recruits on the front lines. They would be worthless in battle.

Clearly, they didn't work well with others, so it makes sense they would hire someone else to do their dirty work for them. Enter the Human Resources (HR) department. As previously mentioned, its creation was two-fold. First, it was introduced to project the illusion of a successfully large, professional business. Second, they needed a channel through which they would dispense all the unpleasant tasks they wished to avoid. They needed employees, they needed customers, they needed people, but they had no desire to interact with any of them.

Richard was a narcissist's ideal subordinate and perfect candidate to head up their personal vendetta campaigns under the prestigious title "Head of HR." There was a love/hate relationship with Richard. The owners even considered firing him for slacking on basic work responsibilities because his mistakes were costing them more money than they wished to calculate. But, he would manage to redeem himself by showering compliments on Karen and Herb, negatively reinforcing their inflated sense of self. They could count on him to be a manager who would never critique their business decisions and would laugh at all their jokes (personal attacks).

Richard truly was a charming and engaging conversationalist who had the ability to make everyone around him feel welcome. He was also the kind of man who found that doing the bare minimum would suit him quite nicely. He would agree to whatever the owners asked if it meant they'd slither out of his office quickly so he could go back to the easy listening of his jazz radio station. The combination of his deep voice and happy demeanor made him perfect for meeting new people. He was so talented that you could hardly tell he was faking it unless you had the opportunity to hear his blasphemous mumbles during moments of weakness.

Richard was someone I enjoyed spending time with until I had the unpleasant realization of what little regard he held for others around him. I had to give him props, though. He wanted to get paid for doing nothing and he was succeeding. He successfully pushed most of his responsibilities onto others, spending more time concealing his mistakes rather than fixing them. I watched day after day as he refused to stick up for the team he oversaw as they endured countless false accusations and criticism from the boss. He confessed that sticking up for his team would "require a conversation with Karen." Simply put, he wasn't going to manage because that would interrupt his day of doing nothing.

In the end, the owner's determined Richard was too well connected to discharge and they needed those connections for the business to stay afloat. Instead, they opted to take responsibility away from him, which he gladly gave up. You didn't have to ask him twice. Who's going to complain about getting paid the same to do less work. The HR department is typically responsible for payroll, benefits, hiring, firing, addressing daily internal issues, keeping up-to-date with state and federal laws, and most importantly, engaging the needs of personnel on a regular basis. However, since delegating was a problem for the owners, those responsibilities were changed to delaying important issues, expediting personal agendas and keeping up appearances of control.

The Abyss
Death by Box

If I wasn't allowed to improve the company's public image on the outside (despite having the title for it), I would attempt to improve the quality of work-life from within. Realizing the owners had little respect for anyone outside their management circle, I had to find someone they trusted who could relay my messages for me. I hadn't worked there very long, so perhaps they just needed more time to see what benefits my contributions and work ethic could make.

Another opportunity for me to prove myself came when I learned how disorganized all the company documentation was. Lost client files were common and when we couldn't find files, we could find appointment dates. When we couldn't find appointment dates, we had irate clients and providers tying up the phone lines simultaneously and a boss who refused to take any of the calls.

Utilizing a customer relationship management (CRM) database to help maintain our clientele information was emphatically denied. This wasn't even a small win Dr. Carter could achieve because Karen made it a financial issue. She rejected the idea even before hearing cost options. I did, however, manage to shift our department from copying every single call intake by hand to using the copy machine! Hardly something I'd consider a grand triumph in my career. I wasn't exactly contributing to a new world order, but no one could argue its value. I'm a bit of a laggard to technology myself but writing everything by hand was alarming in every sense of the word.

My next self-appointed project required me to venture far into the Abyss – the storage room that was avoided by everyone in the office. With files in such disarray, no wonder everyone preferred to maintain large, to-be-filed stacks at their cubicles. Boxes were blocking file drawers, miscellaneous documents had lost their original files, and old client companies (or, should I say, lost contracts) were still taking up prime space. This small room was a dump with spilled papers obstructing a clear pathway on the floor. My guess was that someone tried using a leaf blower to clean up an even bigger disaster.

I put in a request that management hire a company to shred all files we weren't legally required to keep anymore. Request denied. I pushed forward by highlighting all the hazards involved. The room was overflowing to the point where no one could properly find space for new documents and the inability to open filing cabinets that were completely blocked with rubbage. Not to mention, stacked boxes above my head could easily fall on someone. The mess wasn't just impeding our work responsibilities, the room itself was a clear fire code violation. Nonetheless, my request was ignored.

I went dumpster diving anyway and began organizing the Abyss just in case a miracle caused the owners to change their minds. I could see Herb pretending not to watch me from his office as I began filtering through over 12 years worth of scattered client, confidential information.

He eventually approached, telling me not to lift boxes anymore because they could strain my back. Should I even bother mentioning that he waited until I was completely finished before instructing me so? From that point on, I was required to ask a man for assistance despite lifting and unloading boxes with proper form. I may have been the smallest person in the office, but I was probably the only one with safety officer responsibilities in the past as well. Had they not even looked at my resume?

Before the day was over, every male manager was forced to approach me and repeat the same instructions, "Hey, Jen. I'm required to inform you that you're not allowed to lift boxes anymore. Come get me next time you find yourself standing in front of one." We'd then smirk and roll our eyes in unison. The new game in the office became *"Jenny's Little Helper."* No matter how small a box was or if it could be carried with one hand, everyone laughed as a guy rushed to my aid.

> "That's funny. None of the other women were told not to lift boxes. And, I'm pregnant. They're not actually worried about any of us. They are paranoid about someone getting hurt and being sued."
>
> ~ Rose

Almost a year after the original request, Karen finally hired a shredding disposal company but only after I started filling up vacant cubicles with boxes meant for the Abyss.

A strategic eyesore turned out to be the best form of motivation. After all, Karen and Herb didn't want to look unprofessional in the eyes of their occasional office guests.

Grooming Tattletales
He Said That She Said That He Said

Tattletales – It's the creation of minions to do your bidding. Not the cute, little, yellow minions that make funny noises and occasionally speak French. It's the kind of coworker that smiles to your face but talks negatively behind your back; the kind of person who doesn't contribute to a group project but takes credit for all your work. It's the coworker who does every menial task instructed by a superior but avoids assisting fellow colleagues with regular job duties. This is a pretend friend complete with trident and horns – a frenemy. Does that term automatically cause a few names to pop into your mind?

Oscar would regale me with hilarious stories of idiotic office behavior including the development of clones. His two previous managers used to stare one another down through their office windows. They were directly across from one another with subordinates in the crossfire, all witnessing the nonsense between the two. They both kept extensive lists on the other person's activities and offenses. They didn't start out like this until the owners instructed both of them to keep an eye on one another.

It's as if Karen and Herb purchased the worst management books available and read them to one another before going to bed every night. "It says here that competition can be a positive motivational force. Why stop there? We could turn *all* the employees against each other!" So much for encouraging teamwork. "This chapter provides tips on how to avoid employees walking all over you. We can skip this because we've mastered the art of ignoring everyone."

Kelly vs. Oscar

This woman wasn't so clever. She'd keep tabs on everything Oscar was doing rather than assisting him with any work. After a few daunting hours of monitoring, she'd relax at her desk with a *People* or *Us* magazine. The only thing to interrupt her quality gossip columns were the phones constantly ringing. She'd shoot a glare towards Oscar every time as if to say, "Why aren't you doing your job?" She had as much technological knowledge as the owners and didn't even know how to turn on the computer. When that was mastered, next was learning how to turn it off. In between those lessons, she'd walk away from her desk leaving important document windows active on the screen. "Oscar took a long lunch. Oscar came back from lunch late. Oscar is not answering phones." The list went on and on.

> "There it was, an extensive log of my supposed daily activities. Shouldn't have surprised me, though. This is the same girl who tried updating her cell phone at work by using her home Wi-Fi password. They don't exactly hire quality around here. They prefer dumb people they can control."
> ~ Oscar

Kelly was actually creating more work than she was eliminating. After weeks of feeling the stress of constantly redoing everything she touched, Oscar told management how completely unhelpful she was. She didn't understand the basics of anything including human communication or technological skills like her resume claimed. Result? Oscar was accused of lying and they didn't bother checking the truth of his concerns. He never addressed the issues again. He also stopped assisting Kelly and correcting her work.

Arthur

Arthur was an older employee, similar to the owners, which automatically gave him seniority in more ways beyond age. The owner's mistake was sitting their personal friend right outside their corner offices like all their pets before him. He was groomed to keep guard and, once again, keep tabs on us, the outsiders. I may have started out not having any respect for the man, but that didn't mean I would treat him with disrespect. I spoke kindly to him the same way I would anyone else. To my surprise, he turned out to be a gentle soul and a delight to speak with. We enjoyed laughing and challenging one another's intellect, which was an uncommon experience at the office (and a key reason why I personally was falling head-first down Maslow's Hierarchy).

Arthur began to see what happens when dysfunctional management gets ahold of a once thriving business. When his old friends wouldn't listen to him about the staff's need for extra help, he did as the rest of us did. He went straight to Dr. Carter for counsel, skipping HR altogether. It was to her that he spilled the beans about how he'd been instructed to keep an eye on everyone and report back to Karen and Herb with juicy details. He was hired to spend his time spying on everyone in the office. Unfortunately, he found the business in a much different position than he had ever imagined. They were losing pricey contracts, there was no communication with management and the minimal staff was overloaded with more than twice the amount of work appropriate.

I watched as the combination of employee socialization and personal morals caused the poor man to break down and express his concerns openly. You could tell he was new. Company culture demanded that he keep his internal struggles to himself because they were unimportant. It was the first time I witnessed a personal friend of the owner's question their methods. As it turns out, Arthur wasn't a minion. They accidentally hired a great employee who was capable of critical thinking!

Final Thoughts
Chapter 2

With the owners having so many methodological weaknesses and high levels of structural rigidity regarding employee motivation, I was surprised we were still able to help some of our clients. We were accomplishing a few things but not exactly with elegance. We were driving full-speed ahead on a very bumpy road and our tires were going to blow sooner or later. If it weren't for our ability to shrug off a blockade or two (or ten), we would have already been done. The owners of the business may have not valued me, but I was important to the people calling in everyday. Helping them filled my days with purpose. I still had enough energy to stay professional with my clientele. I'd keep them far from the truth. They didn't need to know I had begun hashtagging #OfficeFromHell during my workdays.

If a better job opportunity came along, I'd probably take it. I didn't have much appreciation for the dictator, motivational style that focused on creating opposition within a team. These were good people I was working with. We could achieve so much more together rather than separately.

Identifying a few mistakes:
- Why would you ignore your friends?
- Why do you enjoy inflicting high stress levels?

- Why would you turn employees against one another?
- Why are you still laughing?

BECAUSE YOU'RE NOT DOING IT RIGHT UNLESS YOU'RE DOING IT WRONG!

Chapter

3

ALMOST ENGAGED

Social

I don't feel valued by management, so I slide down the Needs Pyramid in search of comradery amongst my colleagues. *Social* needs of love and belonging rest in the center of Maslow's hierarchy like someone balancing in the middle of a seesaw on the playground. At this stage where commitment to a job is being questioned, tipping the seesaw one-way or the other (even to a minor extent) can have extreme affects on determining an individual's engagement level at work. Will there be a chance for advancement? Am I respected here as an integral part of this business? Am I allowed to contribute to the decision-making process? I'm proud to be a working member of society, but does upper management truly understand my value?

If you find yourself at this stage, you can be sure your employer has half-assed their responsibilities. They've successfully completed all the legal requirements of running a business but failed to acknowledge the human component any further. All the proper manuals were developed and passed out. Everyone knows the procedures and schedules for salary payments, vacation, insurance details, and the complaint/firing procedures. Management can take a big sigh of relief because they've done everything necessary to protect themselves. However, just because they legally earned the right to have employees does not automatically make them true leaders in the *Social* arena.

At the most basic level of Social needs there's the desire for people to connect with those around them, to feel part of something bigger than themselves alone. Considering how much of our lives are spent working, this environment offers ripe opportunities to develop bonds and friendships with our teammates. Through group projects, employees come to rely on one another's skills and individual experiences to solve daily problems. A sense of family is created when members are nurtured during brainstorming sessions, meetings and other social gatherings, all of which make them feel they have a stronger purpose together in numbers.

Rejected by leadership, our needs are now focused on bonding with those around us for a little *Social* pick-me-up. And, nothing bonds people together better than a common enemy. If leadership continuously fails to acknowledge the importance of those around them, management runs the risk of losing commitment from quality employees.

Company Culture Weather Forecast: Cloudy with a 65% chance of leaving work later than anticipated.

Shoot the Messenger
The Unequivocal Suicide Mission

During war or peace, there was never a good time to deliver bad news in this office. Negativity wasn't the only thing shot down either. If you're the one delivering the unfortunate news, you'll get shot, too! Anyone at my office who tries to improve the work environment by addressing real concerns loses out on more than they could ever imagine. It's a tradeoff made every time we would open our mouths. It's also proof that you should never give a gun to a trigger-happy clown.

Bullseye

Dr. Carter is a perfect, target-worthy example. She took a huge loss when she chose to stand up for the rest of the help, a battle she took on single-handedly almost every single day. But, as a manager, she was predestined for failure. After all, it's a manager's duty to keep their superiors apprised of anything relevant that may hinder the company's progress and follow-up with suggestions for improvement. Unfortunately, these leaders couldn't handle the truth if it were deep fried and topped with cotton candy sprinkles like most acceptable treats found at the circus. If, by chance, bad news was accepted, it certainly wasn't because of something *they* did wrong. They were sure it could only be the result of external factors (insert conspiracy theory here). It was always someone else's fault.

As mentioned before, we are not individually defined by what happens to us, but instead, by how we *respond* to what happens to us. If your car collides with someone else's, what's your first response? Do you immediately get out of your vehicle and start screaming at the other driver or do you check to see if they're safe? If a friend arrives late to a happy-hour rendezvous, does your annoyance automatically label them as disrespectful of your time or do you give them the benefit of a doubt and assume their boss kept them late?

We can't always control everything around us but we can control our reactions. The same holds true at work. The way Karen and Herb continuously addressed both the good and bad situations set the tone for all of us who worked for them. The culture threatened anyone with half a brain.

We tried to stop it from happening but our clients were generously showered with the same type of aggressive treatment as we were. You now that feeling of getting the run around from a customer service department over the telephone? You ask a simple question only to be passed from one "experienced" representative to another. Your voice grows louder and louder but still no one hears you. While you're secretly dreaming of their demise, the help line rep is counting on the lapse of time to frustrate you to the point of ending the call early and never contacted them again.

That is exactly how this business was run. All complaints were considered invalid and these complainers were added to a long list of "problem clients" to be ignored alongside any of us that chimed in on their behalf. If you're associated with bad news, you automatically get blacklisted. Questioning Karen's management skills meant she'd retaliate by questioning ours. Next thing you know, someone in the office has become the main character to her newest conspiracy theory and magically, more often than not, they find themselves jobless for undisclosed reasons.

The psychosis unfolds something like this:

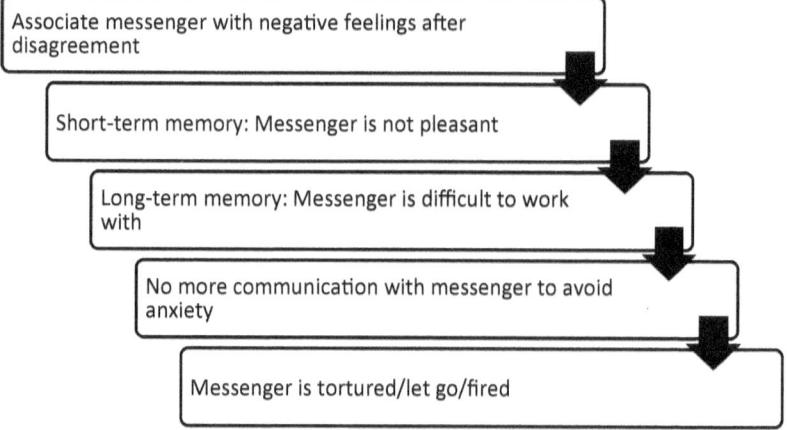

So, what other options did we have? An organization that cares about meeting their financial goals cares about improvement. If they care about improvement, they care about the collective thoughts of their organization. Therefore, it could be reasoned that an organization that cares about meeting their financial goals cares about their whole team. Unfortunately, we couldn't move towards financial success because the owners created a corporate culture that denied improvement at the very basic levels. This was continually drilled into our minds over and over again. If we misunderstood their message, we would pay dearly.

Sensitive Issues

Stacks of case files were growing on my desk for reasons I could not control. I was becoming self-conscious that someone might think I was slacking on my responsibilities even though everyone else's desk looked exactly the same. Nevertheless, I risked speaking with Karen directly. I informed her that it was becoming increasingly difficult to schedule appointments for our clients because more and more providers were choosing not to work with us anymore. She appeared genuinely concerned until I explained why. Counselors of all types were unhappy with the payment cycle. They were receiving a check well over three months after services were rendered! Who could blame them for getting upset?

I knew I hit a sensitive chord when Karen's face changed from pretentiously, pale pink to self-righteous red. As soon as her responsibilities were in question, she downplayed the concerns of my entire department. "We've always had people leave! We just need to find new ones!" This is despite handing her quantifiable evidence supporting the fact that we were running out of professionals to utilize. As a result of her ignoring a huge

Social problem, the hate calls grew louder and the stacks of incomplete files grew taller.

> "You can't expect illogical people to behave in a logical fashion."
>
> ~ Dr. Carter

I thought I was doing my job by addressing a very real threat to our daily operations. Sadly, it turns out there can be negative repercussions to positive intentions as well. What they say is true. No good deed goes unpunished. My attempt to prevent disaster and do the right thing resulted in my excommunication from the house of crazy. The owners completely stopped speaking to me altogether. My bosses stopped all direct communication! Can you imagine trying to run a successful business where you're not on speaking terms with your own people?

Knowing that Karen didn't welcome constructive criticism in any dignified manner, I tried to leave all my personal opinions out of our conversation. Just present the fact and let them decide what to do. But, it didn't matter. By bringing up a factual, financial issue (something they valued more than human beings), I had shed light on their inability to keep the business afloat. All I was trying to do was help find providers for my clients when I should have been obtaining a therapist for my boss.

It was a problem most of the women in the office and I shared – telling the truth. Out of the remaining four managers, two male/two female, the women were the only ones who were honest about what was actually happening at work. The men on the other hand, when confronted with questions regarding any aspect of the business, would lie and stand in yes-man formation. One of them even consistently refused to step beyond the boss's doorway when delivering news of any kind in order to make a quick escape. I highlight these behavioral differences amongst the genders not because I believe all work environments are like this but merely to illustrate how screwed up work environments can become. The truth of the matter is that in this particular situation, the men had been employed longer and had chosen their method of survival long before we had ever come on board.

Lies compounding upon more lies, I saw the men lose focus on the strength that can be found within group cohesion. The team leaders stopped checking on those at the front lines of business operations. They discontinued all casual conversations with us and they couldn't be bothered to help with daily tasks. The combination of avoidance and lies becoming first-nature turned them into managers who were only out for themselves, leaving their subordinates to fight fire-breathing dragons on their own. We no longer had any leaders because focusing on others was no longer management's main priority.

Why wasn't anything working properly?! The *Social* equations weren't adding up. You're ripped apart for telling the truth and rewarded for lying. The most commonplace behavior was anything but common. Nothing made sense. In this eight-to-five psych ward, one plus two did NOT equal three. And, if you said that it did, you'd get shot in the leg and told your health insurance wouldn't cover it.

Penny Pinchers
My Precious!

Maintaining collective salaries of nearly half a million dollars was crucial to the very existence of these business owners. They had a lifestyle to maintain so Herb supported Karen's Scroogy behavior when it came to tightening business expenses. She had a sign-in sheet made for those taking basic supplies from the storage room, she hid the three-hole punch so no one could steal it, and she removed all coffee additives from the morning menu. Simply put: Money matters. People don't. Human beings were paltry compared to the inanimate objects their money could buy.

With the business failing to meet financial goals, the owners saw fit to let another employee go in order to make up the cost. I noticed a clear transition from full-time employees to part-time in the course of my employment. I even began successfully forecasting the lineup of discards.

The Lineup

Poor Brad. He never had a chance. It was easy to forget about him because he sat alone in one corner of the office, head down, hoping not to attract any unwanted attention. He was neither a manager nor a memorable employee. He'd come into the office everyday, do his work and leave, all without saying one word to anyone else. No doubt this was his preferred method of survival, but it also meant he was definitely the next to go. He drained the owner's income as a full-timer and they didn't trust him because he was hired by another person they unceremoniously fired as well.

My prediction was solidified when management began criticizing his work out of nowhere. All of a sudden, after years of performing the same, routine functions, he was abruptly scolded for doing his job wrong. He was accused of filling out paperwork incorrectly, failing to address clients in a timely manner and collecting an insufficient amount of payments, just to name a few. With that, I gave him at least two weeks until the ax came down. I was wrong. He was gone in four days.

This meant my pal, Oscar, was the only full-time employee left who was not a manager. He wasn't next on my list, though. I had the feeling Karen would begin targeting the females next. But, for the time being, they had enough petty cash to maintain their extravagant lifestyle. Plus, Oscar had very important responsibilities that were crucial to keeping the business running smoothly. Or, not.

Your Chariot Awaits

Karen and Herb drove two, bronze, Lexus vehicles that were spotlessly detailed at the office about once a week. The routine was simple. They'd arrive to work and drop their keys off onto Oscar's desk, making it his responsibility to pass on instructions to the cleaner. So, as you can see, Oscar wasn't going to be fired. He was clearly needed to babysit their prized possessions.

Dr. Carter was horrified to see her overworked staff forced to do menial chores and addressed it with a reluctant audience.

What she said: *"Morale in this office is at an all-time low but this can be easily remedied. Unfortunately, there's a negative perception of having to do personal tasks for your boss who isn't paying you well and who continuously denies raises. The perception itself, whether founded or unfounded, is still very real."*

What she meant: *"Stop complaining that work isn't getting accomplished when you have my staff focusing on your own personal errands. These people have been given no reason to dedicate themselves to your success and tasks like these may push them over the edge. You're going to be left with no one to run your company if you keep this up."*

Offended by the accusation that their precious, poop-colored vehicles played any role in dampening the work environment, Karen rages, "What does it matter what we do with our money and if we have them retrieve our keys?! We use our own money to have our own cars detailed! OUR money!" I'm sure Herb would have chimed in with some shit-flavored antidote about employee competence but where did he go? Oh, that's right. He stormed out of the room in the middle of Dr. Carter's caution.

Sticking up for her people was going to cost Victoria dearly. She did the number one office no-no – instructing the boss duo on their personal behavior. She made a personal attack. Victoria was bad. BAD Victoria!

Hitler's Reign
Let the Games Begin

The amount of paranoia in this office was overwhelmingly entertaining. Imagine late night talk-radio meets cult-like religious group. Karen and Herb would run wild with imaginary ideas the same way a child overdramatizes what's in their closet or under their bed. Their ability to connect dots that never exited added a bit of color to a rather dull workday. But, then again, so does drinking, an activity practiced by several of my colleagues during their lunch break. Throw a handful of pathological neurosis into a bag, shake it about and pull one out. You'll get a winner every time!

Do You Have a Business Card?

All of a sudden, the building's maintenance man was looking rather sketchy. Sure, he'd been around for years, but who was he really? Rather convenient for him to claim the only access to the roof was through the office supply room. Was he stealing our (free) company pamphlets? You couldn't be too careful, so Karen instructed everyone in the office to get a business card from every visitor. This would have been one of her more sane demands except for one minor factoid – we didn't get visitors. Even if we did, with client's confidential information sprawled out on our desks everyday, it would have been inappropriate to entertain any. An exception was routinely made, of course, for friends of the owner's who were allowed to walk around wherever they pleased (none of whom gave us the asshole audit we repeatedly requested). Outside of building maintenance, the only regulars included the UPS man delivering boxes I wasn't allowed to carry, the Arrowhead water deliveryman who was in-and-out in less than three minutes and the fax machine tech support. And, the only reason tech support showed up was because the owners refused to spend money on a new fax machine made within this decade.

The fun didn't stop there. Karen was convinced people in the office were tapping into her phone lines. Office potlucks were strictly prohibited because someone may poison the dishes. Not to mention, there was a questionable, lookalike shadow that kept following her around during the daylight hours. Yeah, this was some seriously radicle CIA nonsense. The only thing missing were spaceships and the mention of creating a superior race. (Although, Herb regularly mentioned the need for a superior staff.) Karen would walk into a room and be convinced everyone was talking about her. What had they heard? Did these minions know something they shouldn't? Did they know something she should?

> "Apparently, Jennifer and I are forming a coup – 'a sudden, violent and illegal seizure of power.' We both took the same day off, so Karen spent most of her time asking everyone in the office questions about our relationship. 'I know they're friends. What do you think they're doing together? Do you think they are really sick or just pretending? Did they mention

> anything significant before they left?'"
>
> ~ Elizabeth

Enough on that because someone needs to answer these ringing telephones. A man calls in wanting counseling but hesitates in telling us who he is or what the problem is. Sound the alarm! That's a competitor attempting to gather information that will tear clients away from our company! Or, perhaps, it's a disgruntled ex-employee attempting to tie up the phone lines out of spite or get services they should be paying for. Either way the caller is clearly out to get them. Better play it safe and go back to hiding in the corner office.

Alert! Vulture Overhead

The only time Herb ventured out of his office was to fulfill his daily ego needs by circling the working people like a vulture, lingering in the bathroom or stalking people from the kitchen. The bathroom was for reasons I forever wish to unhear but can't due to husband and wife always yelling into their speakerphones with their doors wide open. Visits to the kitchen, however, were much more interesting.

When an employee was fired or let go, he'd spend over a week walking to and from the kitchen window that faced the parking lot to make sure no one was vandalizing his sparkly, clean Lexus. He was also a self-appointed watchdog lurking over Elizabeth's bi-daily mail check. Retrieving business mail was beneath him but watching someone else walk to and from the mailbox was doable. Watching him watch her creeped everyone out. If she came back empty-handed, the only reasonable response was, "Someone must be stealing our stuff. You should start checking the mail three times a day."

> "Herb is just floating aimlessly around the office like a big fart in a haunted outhouse."
>
> ~ Elizabeth

If Herb wanted to communicate with one of us directly, he chose the intercom over face-to-face almost every time. He'd beep someone's phone from his office, yell his or her name once and proceed to blow air heavily into the speaker for the entire room to hear. If you're not sure what that sounds like, try it with your own office telephone and watch as you quickly lose friends. It was so obnoxious and relatively disrespectful that I had no choice but to ignore my own president and use him as a form of cheap, idiotic entertainment for the rest of my cellmates. They loved anyone who had the nerve to shut down the king and queen.

People with this behavioral pattern either have a clear, diagnosable level of schizophrenia or are simply dishonest at heart. I will allow the psychological professionals to speak about their mental health, but I can touch on their work ethic. Most of the documents created at the top were completely fabricated pieced of art designed to mask a thick layer of poppycock. Intrigued? Read on.

Verbal Vomit
Grab a Mop

Clean up on aisle two, three and probably aisle four! I regularly encouraged my colleagues to keep documentation of inappropriate office behavior but no one was taking me seriously. I couldn't decide if they had never been exposed to the legal aspect of the working world before or if they had given up hope of anything good coming out of something so incredibly bad. And, if that were true, who could blame them? Everyday we were forced to listen to leadership's constant complaining, blaming us for their incompetence. My coworkers probably didn't want to expend more energy on additional paperwork, but they did take advantage of me documenting. To pass the worthless days, my colleagues were able to find joy in regaling me with personal, nightmare worthy stories relating to the owner's personal conduct.

Sex & Zac Efron

Herb did not like large women. The man just couldn't seem to keep thoughts like that to himself. It was always the first comment he made when describing a female. "She's a really big girl… That large woman… The heavy one…" – always expressed in conjunction with the stink eye. Why was my boss so comfortable publicizing himself as an idiot?

To be fair, there's the possibility Herb wasn't attracted to women in general. When Kevin was asked to transfer all of Herb's information from one computer to another, he came across several folders containing explicit images of man on man activity. Trying to pretend like nothing happened, Kevin completed the task and returned the computer as quickly as possible. Herb's awkward explanation only made things worse, "Yeah. So, someone stole my computer and put some porn on it. Sorry, if that popped up." (Phrasing!)

> "Yeah, right. Someone stole your computer and then gave it back. Dear God, get all of this out of my head. Everyday, I cringe at the thought of him needing my help with anything... ever."
> ~ Kevin

Before Kevin had a chance to fully sanitize his brain, Mr. Computer Inept needed his emails forwarded from all his personal accounts to his phone so they were readily available during upcoming travels. As always, Kevin does what he is told and suffers greatly as he sees email addresses that include Zac Efron's name. Why does a grown man need email addresses with a teen, heartthrob's name in it?

Herb's preferred extracurricular activities became topic of conversation once again when his lack of propriety exposed more employees to sexual images. Rose was a kindhearted colleague and mother of five who benevolently advised me with her own confession. Even if Herb's office door was open, she would announce herself long before reaching it to avoid being exposed to unwanted visuals. Following her example, the only thing I was subjected to was Herb quickly minimizing active windows on his computer screen. Others in the office weren't so lucky.

> "Large thumbnails appear with titles. Words like 'butthole' and 'penis' kept appearing. 'Zac Efron bathtub' was another. I put it all on a flash drive like he [Herb] wanted and tried to get out of his office as quickly as possible. Those images cannot be unseen. I don't care how small a thumbnail can get."
>
> ~ Oscar

Let's add to the gender confusion, shall we? Returning from a work event, Herb mentions to Oscar and I that he ran into a provider who knew us. Bursting his little, temperamental bubble, Oscar informed him that we no longer utilized that person because of her unprofessional work ethic. Herb's only response came with laughter, "Well, she's this cute, little, blond thing. So, she's definitely got somethin' goin' on for her," suggestively raising his eyebrows up and down more times than I care to remember. As a petite, strawberry blond, that was too close for comfort for me.

Scenarios of a sexual nature only covered the surface of inappropriate behavior in this office. Herb always made it abundantly clear how incompetent he thought his employees were. "They are small-minded!" was often yelled from the security of his office. If you were younger than he was (which everyone was), the genius would automatically typecast you with another rant, "Ugh! Millenials!" no matter if your age fit the description or not. I can't forget his cheap, personal attacks, either. "Psh. I see you pretending to work, Jennifer. No one types that fast." Well, they certainly don't type 110 words-per-minute with only their index fingers, Herb. Should I have told him he can find porn on his computer a lot faster if he would learn to type with all 10 fingers?

Cook Those Books

Taking advantage of my educational background, Dr. Carter convinced Karen that allowing me to conduct customer satisfaction surveys would be a useful research tool essential for strategic planning in the future. The data could also be added to the utilization reports to show client's how well we were servicing their people. Karen agreed but insisted I only survey people if they seemed happy with the services provided and would give positive responses. The one marketing task I get asked to do and they wanted me to shit all over it. "I will do nothing of the sort. You can do whatever you want with the accurate data I collect, but I will be surveying everyone I can." Put aside my general refusal to perform tasks as directed by a superior, I could've easily been fired for the tone and demeanor of my response.

According to these surveys (that weren't collected from me until after utilization reports were sent to our client companies), we were all extraordinary employees. We met client needs no less than 98% of the time. Don't mind the fact that the number of surveys completed were grossly exaggerated, sometimes by over 400%. Being the nerd that I was (am), I began configuring exactly how inflated the numbers were by maintaining an Excel document I named "BB" – Business Baloney. This revealed one particular instance where only two surveys had been taken but Karen boldly reported 43 as completed, all with raving reviews.

> Oscar: "So, you know how Karen and Herb say we don't do our jobs? Well, these customer satisfaction surveys say differently. Jennifer, we're the best! The [XXX] company loves us!"
>
> Jennifer: "I'm all for becoming the magical unicorns of customer service, but I didn't conduct any surveys with people from that company."
>
> Oscar: "Ha! Of course, you didn't. But, it's documented that we're AMAZING!"

Eureka! That must have been why Dr. Carter was never allowed to take a load off Karen and create utilization reports. I could tell Karen and Herb liked her because she was usually allowed to finish her sentences during a meeting. However, they also thought she was smart enough to see that Karen had taken the liberty of manipulating those numbers and identify how long she had been doing it. She inflated the numbers, stretched them, blew them up. No matter which way you prefer to dramatize cooking the books, she was one lousy chef. We had some client companies whose employees never called in for any services but that's not what the utilization reports said. Zero calls morphed into 20 and 35 calls magically jumped to over a 100.

To add to the entertainment, nothing added up correctly either. If accountants gave an award for the worst book-cooker in the world, Karen would definitely win! Anyone who passed third grade math would realize that WE were paying THEM to use our services. If these numbers were truthful, what we paid out far exceeded what companies paid us.

Final Thoughts
Chapter 3

Statistically quantifiable evidence was admissible if these leaders should be at fault for anything. It's not possible for them to do any wrong. You could put decades of scientifically proven data right on their desks that correlate the profits to be gained by concentrating on employee retention and they would emphatically deny it all. That's there choice, but no one in a leadership position can afford to mock their employees.

There's a reason Karen's name always comes before Herb's. She does, after all, possess complete control over him and, therefore, wears the pants in the relationship. She holds the testicles, rules the roost, cracks the whip. Whatever crass explanation suits you best, it all applies. It's a classic case of insecure woman beats weak man into submission. The working environment they created as a dysfunctional duo was nothing to be proud of.

Perhaps, Karen thought the same methods would work on her employees as they had on her husband. She could control the president of the company so why should everyone beneath him be any different. In an attempt to be objective, I believe business owners should be able to provide employees with whatever (legal) amount of benefits and pay that they wish to. Workers can't expect minimum wage jobs to sustain a full-time living. Just the same, employers can't expect employees to continue working for them when their personal concerns are ignored.

Otherwise, turnover will skyrocket, and they'll lose more money training new people then they would on retention.

How is it that inanimate objects get more attention and care than a human being? When a wheel is squeaky, it immediately gets oil. But, if an employee makes noise at work, management often ignores them, letting their capabilities rust and allowing a buildup of bitter resentment. Losing quality workers eventually leads to a negative bottom line. People are no longer satisfied working for employers who don't value their contributions, and they respond by creating goals that will motivate them to continue forward, goals that have nothing to do with the business. And, if the employees aren't thinking about the business, you've lost them (your human resource), even if they're still physically at their desks.

My working environment was nothing short of unyielding and adverse to growth. I was given no choice but to stop trying to change the culture at the top but focus on improving the daily lives of my fellow teammates instead. I felt beaten down. I couldn't believe I'd been reduced from using my intellect to improve a company's chance of success. Now it was all about our security as individuals. This was the only thing that kept me going even though I wasn't sure I had enough energy on reserve for those battles that were still ahead of me.

Throughout my enthusiastic attempts to contribute, my biggest mistake was assuming everyone was playing by the same rules. I was sure every professional in the working world had similar, universal ideals for things both right and wrong, fact or fiction, good and bad. I've learned my lesson. You can't control crazy. You can temporarily sedate it, but you can't control it.

Identifying a few mistakes:

- Why do you talk more than you listen?
- Why don't you trust anyone?
- Why do you love "yes" men?
- Why would you avoid going directly to the source for answers?
- Why would you punish someone for telling the truth?

BECAUSE YOU'RE NOT DOING IT RIGHT UNLESS YOU'RE DOING IT WRONG!

Chapter

4

NOT ENGAGED

Safety

Falling into the demotivating sections of the pyramid is anything but fun. Employees become disengaged with their daily work and my own struggle to find joy in anything I did was proof of that. My unhappiness was reaching heightened proportions that I had never experienced before, and it was leaking over into my personal life. I thought I was a strong person, perhaps even a leader in times of trouble. So, how could I have let this happen? How could I have let a toxic environment destroy my outlook? When did I go from a positive force to be reckoned with to a time card junkie of ambivalence?

I couldn't improve the day-to-day operations in the office and it was getting to the point where I couldn't help the people calling in for assistance either. My employers were only interested in their own career success that dashed any hopes of contributing to a meaningful cause. The selfishness made me feel dirty. The only thing I wanted to do with the stress balls scattered across my desk was throw them at moving targets. Perhaps, it was time to begin thinking about my own security and open myself up to other job opportunities.

If you've ever shared these feelings, it usually means management's priorities were entirely on the physical establishment of employees and treat you more like robots than human beings. I can see why the majority of Americans continue to be wary of those in leadership positions. The abuse of power seems to never end.

Within the *Safety* stage, there's a high need for consistency that makes us feel secure. In our everyday lives, holding a steady job, having a roof over our head, and acquiring things like insurance provide this sense of security in a world full of chaos. Established laws also contribute to both structure and order. There's security in knowing we have the right to make our own decisions and have a clear understanding of what the repercussions are.

Our careers, work salaries, vacation days, pension plans, and health and benefits packages are all considered staples to our security. They are a constant guarantee in exchange for our hard work and dedication. Everything management chooses to add on to these variables are only considered temporary motivators. Everyone loves getting an extra bonus like a raise or an afternoon off from work. Special acts like this may secure our *Safety* position but they don't necessarily have enough muscle to push us upward and out of this stage.

On the other hand, if these promises are taken away or diminished in one form or another, our sense of *Safety* is quickly shattered. It's that feeling you get when a colleague is overheard whispering words like "downsizing" or "cutbacks." It's gut-wrenching. Anxiety floods our senses because the inconsistency threatens our livelihood.

Company Culture Weather Forecast: Chance of rain and high winds with a drop of nostalgia.

Forever Training
Recruiting Quality From AA

If you find your office quickly being filled with inadequate personnel, it's time to take a look at their avenue of entry – the recruiting department. They're slipping through the company doors much easier than you may think. We have an innate response to appreciate individuals who hold commonalities with us compared to those with more differences. Our similarities bond us because of their familiarity. We comfortably relate with their humor, insight and overall perspective. So, it makes sense that a hiring staff would hire people they like, people who are just like them. And, who emulates the vision of quality and dedication to their work better than anyone else? They do, of course! As a result, mediocrity reproduces like jackrabbits on an island of whoredom. If most of the employees are screwed up, the hiring staff probably is, too (pun intended).

These well-known concepts completely escaped Karen and Herb because they chose to believe explicitly in their own righteous judgment. They would do all the hiring themselves, of course, because that was the best way to look for short-term mediocrity that could easily be manipulated. So, naturally, their quality effort had them hiring people found at Herb's AA meetings.

You're Hired

No matter how diligent we all were, there just wasn't enough staff to handle the amount of work being generated. The owners continued ignoring Dr. Carter's warnings about possible burnouts but finally paid attention to their old friend Arthur. His elevating stress level was becoming so blatantly obvious, I was beginning to wonder if he would have a mental breakdown mid-telephone call. He despised doing mediocre work, and it frustrated him to have piles of unfinished client files on his desk at the end of each day. It went against everything he believed in.

Worried Arthur would quit, Herb interviewed two people to potentially fill one position, thinking that would be enough to quiet any plans for a potential mutiny. The first interviewee was a young girl with limited experience working directly with people but was fluent in Spanish. The second interviewee was an older woman, advanced in years above Karen and Herb. She held multiple masters degrees, worked in the social work arena for decades and also spoke Spanish. Who do you think Herb decided to hire? No time was wasted scheduling the young girl for work the very next day.

Ten minutes before the newbie's arrival, she called in to announce that she no longer wished to accept the position. Raise your hand if you think Herb hired the overqualified woman? What's that? No hands? I can see you're beginning to understand the erroneous standards of this fallacious environment.

Herb throws his hands up in the air shouting, "I give up!" He spent 45 minutes finding someone on a job search website, scheduled an appointment to interview and called that hard work. It would be much easier for him to hire someone from his AA meetings and go back to fiddling on his phone all day. Perhaps, he ran out of people to abuse there.

Oops, You're Fired

For the longest time, Karen was desperately trying to get rid of some women in the office like Elizabeth and Rose. These women wouldn't allow management to manipulate their hours, they documented their overtime and they utilized sick days. By Karen's standards, they were NOT ideal employees. Not to mention, they were both going on maternity leave at the same time. But, since they weren't technically doing anything wrong, how could she safely get rid of these costly workers without having a lawsuit on her hands?

Karen and Herb's favorite strategy was practicing what I like to call legal trapping. This is when a superior uses questionable tactics to create a no-win scenario for their intended victim in hopes of gaining an advantage. The employee could be written up, penalized, or even fired. In this case, Karen wanted these women out of the picture altogether and, with the help of her husband, she would do everything in her power to push them out.

Most of their strategies were poorly conducted like the day I overheard Herb ask Rose to teach him the protocol for greeting new clients over the telephone because... (wait for it)... he forgot. The man who does nothing on a regular basis and has zero respect for anyone he works with all of a sudden wants to learn something from a bottom-level employee. Well, isn't that an interesting turn of events. I'd easily bet a 3M sticky pad that he was lying and up to no good. The owners never admitted to forgetting anything, let alone something so basic as how to answer the phone. I knew poor Rose didn't have a chance. It didn't matter if she replied with the best answer in the world, worthy of a gold medal. They would have made anything up just to jump down her throat and reprimand her. They saw an opportunity when Rose's newborn baby had to remain at the hospital due to complications. They let her go with no opportunity to return to work at a later time because she spent too many days at the hospital with her infant.

As for Elizabeth, they stuck with classic badgering techniques in hopes that she would get so upset that she would just leave on her own accord. Karen successfully made her cry once by belittling her existence. Perhaps, they needed to push the aggression just a smidge further. Instead of thanking Elizabeth for her work, we would hear them say, "Oh! She did her J-O-B! I didn't even know she worked here." This may not seem like a big deal at first glance, but when this public mockery occurs daily, it can weigh a good person down. They were behaving terribly to my new friends, and I felt helpless to stop it.

I felt the same way about sweet Lilly. The newest employee in the office was so happy, eager to learn and enthusiastic for more responsibility. She reminded me of myself when I first started working there. She had a little pep to her step that got people smiling whenever she passed by. Poor thing. She had no idea the fire that would soon be lit under her desk chair. I gave myself two options. I could successfully train her the same way I had the last four people before her or I could alter my introduction a bit. I felt like I was about to pop a child's balloon.

Jennifer: "Hey, Lilly. Before we begin going through the training manual, there are some things you should be made aware of. Normally, I prefer giving new employees time to adjust to a new work environment so they can develop their own opinions about the office and find a rhythm of their own. But, unfortunately, I've learned that new hires don't have that luxury here. The luxury of time, that is. So, with your permission, I'd like to give you a few pieces of advice."

Lilly: "Uh, yeah. Absolutely!"

Jennifer: "I am so sorry, but there is nothing I can do to protect you from being let go or fired for no legitimate reason. I can, however, expedite the enlightening process that may provide you with a little more time to get your affairs in order. You've been hired into a toxic work environment where you hold absolutely no value to management except answering that phone and keeping angry clients at bay. They don't appreciate lateness, anyone who utilizing sick days or those who announce personal opinions. So, if you have suggestions on how to improve anything at the office, I'd keep them to yourself because they'll take it personally. If you wish to continue working here, I'd suggest complimenting them often and laughing at their jokes."

Lilly: "I'm a little scared now."

Jennifer: "Oh and you should probably not sign your name on anything they give you and document everything that happens during the workday. Now then, let's take a look at this training manual."

I was pleased that despite my harsh reality check, Lilly picked up the daily routine faster than any other trainee. It didn't matter, though. She was let go a few days later. The owners said they needed someone who could work in the mornings and Lilly was starting school soon. When Dr. Carter probed further, reiterated that Lilly was willing to switch her classes around in order to accommodate, Karen got flustered and blurted out, "This is non-negotiable! I don't have to explain myself!"

> "They originally told me I was guaranteed at least 20 hours a week of work and they were more than willing to work with my school schedule. They seemed so kind and were so excited to have me there. And, I was excited, too! Then, the next thing I know, I'm being quickly escorted out of the building as if I had done something terribly, terribly wrong."
>
> ~ Lilly

DEATH OF THE COMPANY

A few hours later, I was training a new person. Lilly only took a few days to learn the ropes but this one was going to take a few weeks. On top of that, she was working the exact same part-time hours as Lilly had supposedly been let go for. The only difference was this girl was bilingual. She may not have been a quick worker but she picked up on social cues well enough. Only a week goes by before she whispers, "I'm not sure I'm going to stay here very long. I'm not feeling this place. Did you know Herb asked me during my interview if I was going to have children? Apparently, maternity leave has been a problem in the past."

Farewell Friend
Dare to Dream

Oscar put in his two weeks notice. He found a job where the leadership valued his abilities and he would soon begin enjoying his workdays for the first time in a long time. He had rescued himself and we were jealously happy for him. Not being a complicated person, Oscar's resignation letter was simple and straightforward. "Hi, I'm resigning. My last day will be two weeks from today."

> "You know when a chicken looks around in 100 different directions? That's probably the best description of Karen's panic when I told her I was leaving and never coming back again."
>
> ~ Oscar

Karen starred at the letter for about five minutes, then grabbed her pad of sticky notes and ran to the clinical director's office for a constructive chat with Victoria.

Karen: "Did you know Oscar was going to leave?"

Dr. Carter: "Yes."

Karen: "Why didn't you tell us?!"

Dr. Carter: "Because every time I tell you something that's going to happen, you and Herb get upset with me and tell me that it's not true. You get mad and don't trust me, and I'm tired of being treated that way."

Karen: "Oh, that's not true. We trust you."

Dr. Carter: "No, you don't. You even told me."

Karen: "Well, whose side are you on? Theirs or ours?"

Dr. Carter: "I'm a manager, Karen. I'm on both sides."

Promotional Me

I was missing Oscar before he was even gone. He was this immoveable force that regularly stumped the owners, rendering them inoperable. He taught me so many important things like how to say no to your boss, how to let inappropriate comments roll off your shoulder and how to lighten up the work day by watching an episode or two of *Drunk History* at our desks. He had influenced my life in a positive way, and I was proud of the work he had accomplished despite all the odds against him.

With Oscar leaving, I knew the owners would be scrambling to find someone who could fill his place. Their easiest option was to have me absorb his responsibilities, which was hilarious since I knew how much they disliked me. They may have hated me, but they were going to need my help. But, what are you supposed to do when the devil is proud of the work you've done and wants to give you a pat on the back?

Karen called me into her office to inform me that I was getting promoted to a full-time position. Jump for joy? I was sitting silently before she mentioned the raise I'd receive with my new job - $1.50 an hour. I burst out laughing and tried to recover quickly by pretending to cough. The offer was comical to say the least. So was her surprised face when I asked for time to think it over. She was clearly annoyed I was stalling her master plans.

The next morning, I declined her offer. I declared that the raise would convince me to stay in the current position but it wasn't tempting enough to convince me to take on more work. As the most qualified person in my department, I was the frontline leader in determining customer care, training new personnel, representing the company during presentations offsite and I would easily be absorbing management responsibilities as well. The opportunity cost was too high, and I'd be giving up the only thing I still had left – my flexibility.

If Karen didn't already hate me, she definitely did after that conversation. She found me ungrateful and my words offensive. But, I was offended, too. I couldn't justify selling my soul for a meager $1.50. I was supposed to do more for less and the devil didn't even offer me my own pitchfork! How rude.

Birthday Wishes
So Let It Be Written, So Let It Be Done

The written word is powerful beyond measure. Ask Shakespeare, Martin Luther or even God. That guy wrote on stone, so you know He wasn't kidding around. This method of communication is difficult to erase from history (if not 100% unlikely thanks to the "Reply All" button within our emails). So, we must think twice about our words before projecting them onto paper for the world to see.

The public is not privy to all written documents, however. Remember having a journal when you were younger? Did you ever get in trouble for passing handwritten notes to friends during class? Can you think back to the days of writing personal snail-mail complete with an actual stamp? Ancient history, I know. But, good times, right? Such a lovely, personal touch that was so safe and secure.

Evil Mailman

I remember the first day some business mail came my way. It was hand-delivered by the president himself. This struck me as an oddity considering the only thing Herb ever delivered was bad news. I would have been amazed by his ability to have normal, human interactions but was far too distracted by all the opened envelopes lying on my desk. He had gone through every single piece of my mail. I picked them up one by one to find the top part of each envelope mutilated by someone's inpatient fingers trying to rip them open. I felt unjustifiably exposed. My privacy had been violated and my anger was surfacing much faster than normal. I sat at my desk starring at my stack of mail and trying to keep my emotions in check. Should I even be feeling this way? Is an owner allowed to go through their employee's mail at work? It *is* his business, I suppose. But, it was *my* mail, addressed to me!

"Yeah, they do that with my mail, too," Dr. Carter attempted to console me. She wasn't helping. "Actually, they do that with everyone's mail." Still not helping. I didn't even know my rights but it was of little matter. She suggested I let it go because there were other battles to be fought. I never received much mail, so I conceded not to push the issue. However, I would wash my hands after reopening the envelopes. I felt gross. I didn't just feel angry and undervalued. I felt physically dirty because I didn't want to be touching anything Herb had touched (for reasons found back on page 86).

Happy Day

A few days before someone's birthday, Karen would have a card circulated amongst the office for signing. This isn't out of the ordinary in a work setting. But, is it typical for the boss to be the last one to sign so they can read what everyone else wrote? Annoyed with her constant need for control, we decided to get a little more creative with our messages. We couldn't even tell our colleagues happy birthday without being monitored, so we decided to make things more interesting. Feeling rather ambitious, Kevin wrote, "La muerte de la empresa!" Thank you, Google Translate. I personally enjoyed tossing in a classic, disgruntled haiku here and there.

> "Smoke signals rising.
> Spectacles required now.
> Perpendicular."
>
> "Free choice in new year.
> Reconstruction of innards.
> Happy Birthday, Man."
>
> ~ Jennifer

I don't know why I insisted on doing that. It only reminded everyone how much of a nerd I was.

Next thing you know, Karen races into HR's office spouting the usual questions. "Why did Kevin write his message in a different language? What does it mean? Is he talking about *this* company? Is he angry with us? Does he have it out for me and Herb?" This wasn't the first time my poems failed to get the attention they so obviously deserved. I mean, the quality, the craftsmanship and the eloquent arrangement of spiteful words. If I hadn't been so busy laughing at Karen's spastic movements in HR's office, I'd pretend to be more offended that my friend's straightforward, blasphemous declaration got all the fuss. But, out of all Karen's questions, she never asked Kevin any of them.

Fast-forward a few months later to Kevin's own birthday as employees pass around yet another generic card void of any humor, sentimental worth or human feeling. Even though Oscar no longer worked with us, he asked Elizabeth to write something on his behalf. In classic, Oscar-style he had her put, "Have a good summer. Love, Oscar." That's all it took to start the witch's cauldron boiling. Here I was writing elaborate poems while masterful Oscar was simplifying the pot-stirring ingredients. I still had so much to learn from him.

Like clockwork, Karen jumps over to the HR's office spouting off the usual questions. "Who wrote this? I think it's Elizabeth's handwriting, but what does it mean? Why would she write a message from someone who doesn't work here anymore?" By the time the birthday card reached its intended victim, Karen had put a mailing label over Oscar's personal message and wrote her own on top. Once again, not one of Karen's questions were ever addressed to Elizabeth herself.

> "It's like our work area is North Korea and all outsiders are evil! I don't even know how to explain how weird she is. I simply grabbed a pen and rewrote Oscar's message again."
>
> ~ Elizabeth

Final Thoughts
Chapter 4

Replacing the people is probably the most common action taken to solve internal business issues, but it rarely solves anything. Management has just found new employees to practice the same mistakes on that are encouraged by the same leadership staff who hold the same self-seeking motivations.

I couldn't tell if these owners cared about anyone but themselves. They hired and fired (to illegal standpoints) anyone at will, so they clearly didn't care about their employees. They refused to pay providers in a timely manner, so there was no respect for those people. Clients were treated well until their money was collected and then the priority was back to finding more people to take money from.

Overwhelmed by all the catchpenny nonsense, I could now see their original basket of offerings only held empty promises in the form of bureaucratic weight that would drown any business that ignorantly thought one plus two actually equaled three. They had a list of priorities and none of us made the cut. Only their needs (and, of course, the needs of their farm animals) were important. Their selfishness was going to cost them everything but a golden parachute. It was us, the people actually working, who would truly end up with nothing.

To make matters worse, I didn't even realize how physically sick I was constantly getting with two days here, three or four days there. The absentee hours were racking up but I couldn't pinpoint exactly why? Had I contracted Mono? No. My lack of love life guaranteed that wasn't a possibility. Had I reverted back to college-style eating habits? Nope. I was still in fairly decent shape for having a desk job. Although, I never experienced the freshmen-15 (the number of pounds gifted to most new college females), the 20-pound desk jockey seemed more palpable.

If all the usual health gauges were normal, what was wrong with me? I could only think of one last possibility, one culprit that I didn't want to admit a weakness to. I had been mentally beat down. More specifically, my mind was not at ease with my environment and I was beginning to show it. My conscious positive attitude couldn't override my true feelings. I tried reminding myself the value in helping others while my subconscious was simultaneously screaming at the owners for not letting me do just that. I was unhappy and felt helpless that there was little I could do to stop sliding down further still.

> "Unfortunately, this kind of thing happens all the time whether we like to admit it or not. The mind is much more powerful than we give it credit for. People usually associate the mind with mental health and disregard the powerful role it plays in our physical health as well. Experiencing sadness, depression or having an increase in anxiety for an extended period of time is a recipe for sickness. The body is a mirror of those feelings that we should never ignore."
> ~ Dr. Carter

Wouldn't it be easier to just give in, to succumb to these conditions and greet depression peacefully? What's wrong with taking the road most traveled, anyway? What would happen if I accepted it? These kinds of questions push me into a flash-forward that quickly answered each one. If I gave up, I'd become *that* girl. She's easy to spot, too. I'd be that girl who always plays Facebook games on her computer rather than decreasing the stack of "To Do" files on her desk; that girl who stores full-sized candy bars in her desk drawer rather than the fun-sized ones; that girl who drinks heavily during her lunch break rather than being the comforting soul who provides gum to all the other self-loathing companions who gave into the temptation.

Nope! Forgive the dramatics, but I choose life. I would press forward like a miniature bulldozer blaring "Move Bitch, Get Out Da Way" from the stereo system. I would reframe my approach and admit to myself that I was using all my energy to improving something that could not be improved. My efforts were admirable, yes, but they were no longer wise. I had to focus on myself before it was too late.

The rest of the office staff had perfected their self-preservation techniques. Not caring whether the business lived or died protected their mental wellness and helped conserve what little energy they had left. It was complete emotional detachment. It was time to become one of them.

Identifying a few mistakes:

- Why do you view employees as disposable products?
- Why wouldn't you try to keep the good employees from leaving?
- Why don't you ever go to the original source for information?
- Why do your birthday cards suck?
- Why don't you like my poems?

BECAUSE YOU'RE NOT DOING IT RIGHT UNLESS YOU'RE DOING IT WRONG!

Chapter

5

DISENGAGED

Physiological

If people are splashing around in a desperate search for a life preserver, the demotivating stages are only getting worse. Here you'll find your scholastic and career dreams lying destitute on the floor like a hamster that's been overworked on the running wheel. You're so focused on your *Physiological* needs that there's no real purpose to your existence at work except getting through the day-to-day. You've become completely disengaged from the tasks at hand because stress overwhelms your thoughts of whether or not your next paycheck will cover your living expenses. You now live for the weekend.

If you or your team members are at this stage of survival, it usually means leadership has failed… at everything. You are only there for the money and will leave the first chance you get. Some will even sacrifice pay for a more positive, fulfilling work environment. (Despite what countless leaders believe, monetary perks are typically only a short-term incentive and hold little value for long-term motivation compared to other variables.) Forget feeling undervalued because you're not valued at all. You've accepted your position and role as a pawn until you can muster up the courage to reconstruct the dreams you used to have.

Such helpless feelings would normally disgust you but you're too exhausted or numb in self-preservation mode to care. This explains the two-fold effect of demotivation: 1) You're ashamed to find your own performance levels falling dramatically, and 2) you sadly don't care anymore that it has intrinsic, negative effects on others around you.

Instead of looking at people, you're looking at clocks. That damn thing never ticks fast enough! Rather than engaging with others, you now prefer the company of inanimate objects like your computer, colorful 3M sticky pads and the miniature dartboard on your desk. You opt to take all breaks outside of the office, extend bathroom visits longer than your bowels find necessary and because budget cutbacks took away your coffee creamer, there's no reason to commune in the lounge either. If you look up from your desk long enough to find the hidden alcoholics returning from their lunch, be kind enough to pass them a stick of gum. But, please, don't expect them to socialize.

As for the *Physiological* needs met by your employer, the office air is semi-breathable and the water cooler is not empty. An obnoxiously slow applause should be awarded to each person on your leadership staff for accomplishing the legal minimum. Rather unrealistic don't you think? They provide only minimum support while expecting maximum output. That's another equation that doesn't make sense.

The lack of enthusiasm in your phone voice makes the entire room keenly aware of how tired and apathetic you are. You can't even be bothered to pack a healthy meal anymore. You just refill the mini bar in your bottom desk drawer with fast food items conveniently available at the local gas station.

Your work calendar, once filled with appointments and noteworthy tasks to accomplish, is now blank with the exception of a red marker X-ing out each, dismal day. You're counting down, but for what? The weekend? Your next paycheck? The unlikely Christmas bonus? Short-term goals are still goals, right? You're not a complete loss. However, becoming a well-rounded human being who can reach *Self-actualization* is the last thing on your mind. Not to mention, helping your boss reach company goals lost its appeal long ago. Getting out of bed in the morning and fixing your hair is a huge accomplishment. Now, the priority is focused only on survival.

Company Culture Weather Forecast: Heavy thunderstorms with a high chance of flooding and an increased chance of suicidal thoughts.

Self-Preservation
The Deterioration of Middle Management

There was a time when people would stick up for one another; a time when noble acts took less energy to perform. I remember when everyone hung out together outside of the office as well as inside. However, the more people that began putting themselves first, the more they lost sight of all the benefits found within group efforts.

Sitting at my desk, barely able to hold up my own melancholy posture, I sensed something different in the air. I could hear the normal sounds of my squeaky chair, faxes not going through, reluctant fingers dialing telephone numbers. There were smells of burnt coffee and stale dreams that confirmed I was still in the same place but something else was missing.

I had seen it before. Employees come into a new workplace with such a high level of enthusiasm that would motivate floors of workers with energy to spare. They jump right in, just as I had, ready to be involved and make a difference. Then they get pushed down (the pyramid). The only difference now was that it was happening to me. I had never felt like this before—completely worthless. I was surrounded by office zombies—half-functional human beings with only the purpose of survival. We weren't dead but close enough.

Middle management, who used to acknowledge the daily struggle and stick up for our efforts, had backed into their emotional hole in hopes of finding sanctuary from the accumulation of human sorrow. They willingly took a seat on the bench and only yelled directions from behind a closed door. Working amongst the toxicity for too long fogged the air around us and they could no longer see clearly. They became temperamental and began lashing out default phrases like, "It's your job. Just do it," and "I'm not getting fired over something so stupid. Get it done." It's comparable to when parents become so exhausted with their children that instead of explaining why certain decisions are made, they exclaim with a huff and a puff, "Because, I said so!"

> "As the last manager standing up for good, I felt responsible for the people we worked with, a kind of kinship. I was afraid to leave them alone with the owners because I knew none of the other managers would help them. I probably would have left my job sooner had I not felt the need to stick by my troops. I was afraid of what would happen to one of them if I left them behind."
>
> ~ Dr. Carter

I don't know where I was finding pockets of strength, but I still tried to find a way to lighten up the workdays for everyone. One gloomy afternoon, as soon as Karen and Herb left for the day (earlier than everyone else was the usual routine), I surprised everyone by pulling out a bowling set hidden underneath my desk. It may have been a child's toy but for a solid half hour, we were laughing and cheering like fresh air had blown back into the office. I kept score and, thanks to the dollar racks conveniently stationed inside Target's front entrance, I even had a bag of prizes for the winners. There were a few brief moments when I recognized signs of life again. It was lovely but short-lived.

The fun was intrusively interrupted by word from my colleague keeping post by the window. "The witch rides again!" she hollered, indicating Karen had decided to come back to the office. In almost perfect rhythm, everyone begins erasing any sign of unusual activity. I managed to catch all the plastic bowling pins tossed my way. All except for one. It hits my head, but I compose myself quick enough to throw everything back into an empty Xerox box. The air in the office went from breathable to stuffy in a matter of seconds as if someone had managed to smack the reset button, but we were successfully going about our business the moment Karen walked through the door. We would live to play another day.

Liar, Liar
Fire

Vagina Penalty

Aggressive, stubborn, unfriendly, bitchy. Thanks to Karen, every negative adjective people are often heard females in a position of power is true. And here, in its perfectly twisted psychosis, is another example for them to use. She's intolerant of differing opinions, won't share company plans, refuses to collaborate with others, openly questions people's motives and the list goes on and on.

I shake my head when forced to grasp the repercussions I'll personally have to deal with as a woman because of Karen's behavior. It's one thing for a man to publically voice negative stereotypes of female leaders, but when a woman proves men right by bringing down other women, it's just embarrassing. Even her husband, Herb, made a few comments suggesting she doesn't get along with other females. In her mind, they were always her biggest threat.

> "My last [female] supervisor came into work one day wearing hiking attire. Seeing her with a hat on, Karen goes straight into her office and instructs her to take it off because it wasn't appropriate work attire. This is even though every single guy in the office, including me, wears one almost every day. No one has ever told us to stop wearing them."
>
> ~ Oscar

When Karen realized her lack of financial management skills were beginning to show, she looked for a quick fix. This frantic search for funds to cushion a dying business had her meeting with the female managers to announce that their work hours were being cut. They had to compensate their financial loss somehow which meant these women's pay would be cut by 25%. The rest of the managers (all male) would stay as they were. Naturally, the women were concerned about the stability of their employment and Elizabeth, a newlywed and first-time homeowner, verbally questioned the new hours of work. She asked if they were going to be flexible with the hours just in case she had to get a second job to support herself. Response, "Oh, no, no. Absolutely not!" The very next day, Karen realizes no manager would be in the office to close at the end of the day. She didn't want to ask the men to adjust their schedules so she sent HR to tell Elizabeth she had to... again.

Why did Karen prefer working with males so much over females? Wouldn't a woman appreciate having someone else they could relate with in the office? Then again, other females in the room would be more keenly aware of the errors and motivations behind her thought process and actions. Men, on the other hand, were at a disadvantage because there are unwritten, social rules about how they can and cannot conduct themselves around a woman both physically and conversationally. So, they told her what she wanted to hear (usually to the point of lying) versus the female managers who were always identifying what was actually going on in their divisions. Voicing the truth meant we had questioned the safe world Karen took a long time mentally building for herself. As a result, women at this office didn't survive very long. There was a female before Karen's time who was running the business with Herb, but Karen phased her out as quickly as she could. Understanding all of this information had me pushing my own exit strategy plans into high gear before one was forced upon me.

Rubble for Sale

The next morning I found a few colleagues hovering over a computer. Sadly, they weren't watching Comedy Central like I had hoped. Instead, they were discussing an advertisement they found announcing the sale of a business—our business to be precise. The owner's desperation had finally surfaced and it was officially public knowledge on one of the Internet's largest business-for-sale sites.

We knew things were going downhill because we were losing clients faster than a compulsive gambler loses their casino chips. The inability of the owners to differentiate company goals with their own personal goals made sure of that. When confronted with the ad, Karen's irritated response was simple, "No, we are not selling the company." Herb's lie took a different approach with, "It must have been one of our competitors that put up the ad."

After a few days of hearing the whispers get noisier, a flustered Karen storms out of her hole to stop all the chatter. "The business is not being sold! You cannot sell a nonprofit!" As if enough ignorant things had not already been said, she proceeds to expose herself further by vomiting more unnecessary information. "The building doesn't even belong to the business! It belongs to us. Karen and Herb own this building. Karen and Herb rent the building to the business." I sat through the rant shaking my head. Our bosses were making even more money than they were legally required to state publically by nonprofit regulations. They found a loophole by using a synthetic lease to siphon money out of the business into their personal bank accounts.

Karen was scared they would lose their labor force. Poor thing was like one of those rubbery kid's toys where the eyes pop out when you squeeze it. It would have been fun watching her get all twitching once again if the pitch in her voice hadn't reached Chihuahua-like proportions and she had stopped referring to herself in the third person. But, then again, she should be scared. After all, if they lost their employees, who would turn on the lights in the morning? Who would change the large Arrowhead water jugs when they were empty? Who would tie their shoes and save their same-sex porn from a dying computer? More importantly, who would take their calls? Who would transfer all irate clients to their voicemail? What on earth would they do if the only legitimate part of their business, the employees, left them?

Taking our silence as tacit compliance, Karen headed straight back into her office after the enlightening speech was over. There was no time made for questions and concerns from the peanut gallery. As far as she was concerned, the issue was closed.

For everyone else, however, the topic was fair game. Calls flooded in with inquiries about our company's status. Were we still open for business? Were Karen and Herb still the owners? Was new management taking over? I even had someone call in pretending to be a student doing a research paper on community focused businesses like ours and needed status information. The questions were growing oddly specific. The ad seemed to bring less opportunity and more fear that caused Karen's twitching and chicken-like mannerisms to return.

W-2

Tax season was creeping up like it always does and I asked Dr. Carter to help me with my paperwork. She agreed but first I needed to procure another copy of my W-2 because I had lost my original like some veteran newbie. A few weeks later, I find that she was able to grab the document from Karen directly. I was comfortable with Dr. Carter having it since we had previously discussed it, but I was greatly disturbed that Karen never checked with me first before passing it out.

Me: "Karen, I understand from Dr. Carter that you gave her a copy of my W-2 form for tax purposes."

Karen: Stares at me like a deer into the headlights... with a slight twitch.

Me: "Next time, because you're the holder of the legal document, would you please check with me first before passing that over to someone else?"

Karen: Visibly shaken, "I don't know what you're talking about. I've never given out your W-2 to anyone!"

Me: "Karen, you're the only person who holds those financial documents and issues them. Why, then, does my W-2 say 'Employer Copy' on it?"

Needless to say, the discussion didn't last very long. She denied any responsibility without providing any alternative to how my confidential information ended up in the hands of someone other than me without my permission. No matter how obvious it was, she had no intention of admitting to anything. The only intention she had was to get me out of her office as quickly as possible. Then a later thought struck me as even more horrifying. If she was comfortable lying about something so blatantly true, what else was she comfortable doing with my personal information?

Happy Friday the 13th
I Quit

Oh, glorious day! I hate admitting this, but I spent roughly 11 months being naïve and another 11 months being angry. I remember the day I walked into the office already in a bad mood, unusual behavior for me to express so openly. My coworker greeted me with a sheepish grin. "Finally," he said. "Welcome." He quickly recognized that I no longer had faith in the environment I spent over a year attempting to improve. He cheered me up by playing one of our favorite games, "Remember When," that required no response but giggles.

Remember when you looked forward to coming into work?

Remember when you thought your boss cared about what you said?

Remember when they lied to our faces?

Remember when people used to open up your mail?

Remember when your boss used to talk to you?

That last one was a new development. The owners wouldn't even look at me anymore, let alone speak words to me. According to my coworkers, I intimidated them, a concept that continues to boggle my mind to this day. All I did was honest labor. But, I suppose, the world is becoming so fake that the truth found in reality actually makes them uncomfortable. Then again, maybe they *should* feel intimidated. There are few things scarier than a small woman going ape-shit, and I knew it was time to take things a step further.

It's always best to resign from a position with as much grace and tactfulness as you would performing any other work-related task. Timing is everything. "Don't burn a bridge when you're only halfway across it," my mother used to say. When is the right moment to quit? In a case such as mine, as quickly as humanly possible. Type "how to quit my job" into any internet search engine and you'll be overwhelmed with the amount of articles available. But don't fret because they all give the same advice. Several of them are even bullet pointed for those desperately scanning for a quick escape.

How to quit your job…

- Notify your boss in person.
- Write a resignation letter thanking and expressing gratitude to the employer.
- Provide plenty of notice.
- Offer to help with the transition of someone taking your place.
- Clean up your work area.
- Ask for a recommendation.

~ General Comments Courtesy of the World Wide Web

Instead of doing something so classically boring, how about I yell at them in front of everyone instead and key their beloved vehicles on my way out while videotaping the whole thing in order to post it on YouTube so the whole world can press replay. There's no doubt that I'd be providing much needed entertainment for the entire staff but that would really serve as the only purpose. Sorry to disappoint, but I'm not that bold.

True to form, like a good, little, close-minded millennial, I did everything I was supposed to—almost. I wrote a resignation letter on company stationary but indicated only the date I would be leaving, not the reason and definitely not conveying any thanks or good wishes. A copy was addressed to each owner and manager. In an environment where no mutual respect was ever intentionally created, 24-hours was plenty of notice, right?

As for my desk area, I couldn't possibly leave a mess so I cleaned everything spotless. No document could be found out of place. Actually, no document could be found at all because everything I created that the owner's communicated was of no value to them in any way (training manuals, presentations, promotional flyers) were fed to the shredding machine, an activity they had me perform regularly. (I embraced this daily, demeaning task because it was stress relieving. They loved having me shred at the end of the day because they could easily have copies of their falsified utilization reports disposed of.) This was all done a few days prior to giving notice just in case I was dismissed immediately, a right they enforced more often than not. And considering compulsive liars don't typically give glowing reviews of ex-employees, I didn't bother asking for a recommendation.

On my way out, my final act of defiance was changing my computer's desktop background to an image found in the movie *Inglorious Bastards* where Christopher Waltz's Nazi character is pointing down to a telephone. You remember, the part near the end where he is asking help from the exact people he was willing to kill just a few moments before. Rather fitting, don't you think?

All the generations before mine would die of shock at such a questionable exit. How completely unprofessional my departing behavior was. Where was my professional courtesy? Where was my respect? There's a good chance those may have been shredded, too. I would rather risk going broke than help the self-involved establish a 401K for their farm animals while continually ignoring the very legs their business and livelihood was standing on. I would rather have Sallie Mae (or whoever is capitalizing on education debt now-a-days) chasing me through the desert sands of the Sahara than help the modern day Scrooges of the world fulfill their dreams of dominance until death. No doubt this attitude was one reason why Herb hated millennials so much. We're so fickle that way.

Dethroned
Hostile Takeover

After a year of desperately seeking a cash rescue, the owners finally found an investment firm willing to provide assistance in stabilizing their crumbling business structure. Herb was so proud of himself about this deal that he ignorantly instructed the office to show the new liaison everything. "The good, the bad and the ugly." So, everyone did just that. Permission was granted by the president himself to unleash every bottled-up truth they'd worked so very hard to ignore.

> "When people get so intense and their lies get so deep, they start truly believing their own lies. They tell themselves that nobody is ever going to figure it out. To them, the lies have actually become the truth."
>
> ~ Dr. Carter

When the liaison from the investment firm learned about the poor company image, the huge contracts that were lost, the poor morale, the inflated utilization reports and the inappropriate behavior and narcissistic views of the owners, he was dumbfounded. He took copious notes and the only response he could mutter was, "I need to speak with my head office."

This deal was moving forward under the agreement of a handshake. No official contract had been signed yet. However, a gentleman's agreement assumes there are gentlemen on both sides of that handshake. To Karen and Herb's dismay, the final contract had some revisions, the biggest one in particular – they were being booted-out. They were no longer to be a part of daily business operations. They were to be stripped of their reach and power. The legal ramifications of their continued presence had the rear end of this business flashing the public. They had to leave and it had to be quickly.

To build a kingdom from a pile of rubble, a hostile takeover was in order. And, what's one of the first things you do to improve a toxic working environment? You remove the source of toxicity threatening success. Reaching peak performance by attaining *Self-actualization* was never going to be possible with Karen and Herb hanging around.

To add to their humiliation, the new president learned about the work I tried to accomplish and immediately began pushing those ideas forward. Internally, CRM guidelines would be created to make catering to client needs more satisfactory for everyone involved. To repair damaged relationships with individual providers that worked with our company, strict payment schedules would also become mandatory.

Externally, the company would immediately begin the process of rebranding. Trust had to be gained back from the public and that wasn't going to happen with Karen and Herb still on their thrones. Not to mention, old services would be eliminated to make room for new ones that would make the business competitively appealing to its target market.

The new leadership team had their work cut out for them. Everything needed to change drastically because the old business was built on quicksand. It was destined for failure from the very beginning because the foundation was faulty to its very core. This company was completely dead.

Final Thoughts
Chapter 5

I feel as though I belong in a classic Disney scene where I prance through grassy meadows of dandelions with victorious glee and jubilation. The young woman who overcomes the trials and tribulations of generational stereotypes, emotional abuse and career malnourishment managed to find the courage to stand up for what she believed in and fight back. I was Mulan (hardly).

I desperately want to proclaim that there's no wrong way to leave a toxic work environment. I want to say that giving an *Office Space* beat down to the company copy machine will solve all your woes. I want to support *The Devil Wears Prada* attitude of ignoring your boss by throwing your work phone into a fountain. However, I can't say that there's nothing wrong with a *Fight Club* mentality of burning down an office building. It's not so much about wrong or right (except that last one doesn't look so golden) as it is about gaining an advantage or disadvantage in a given situation. When it comes time to call a quits, take the time necessary to prepare for departure.

According to Maslow's *Hierarchy of Needs*, true growth towards *Self-actualization* cannot be achieved until you've satisfied the criteria of all four levels below, giving the impression that you're not really happy until you've suffered through the hike from hell with a boss from hell as your special companion. This could not be further from the truth. Happiness, a sort of mental equilibrium, is about the process of moving forward rather than standing still. You can enjoy this by always meeting your simple, everyday goals. Reaching *Self-actualization* is the stage that provides an environment where you are unhindered to accomplish these personal goals rather than the lower levels that distract you with other needs. Not to sound like a self-help book, but take conscious steps forward. Standing still or even stepping backwards is a personal choice we all make every day, multiple times a day, and they can be very tempting.

Identifying a few mistakes:

- Why would you think people would always follow your idiosyncratic rules?
- Why would you forget who keeps your business afloat?
- Why burn a bridge that you're only half way across?
- Why do you insist on giving leadership a bad name?

BECAUSE YOU'RE NOT DOING IT RIGHT UNLESS YOU'RE DOING IT WRONG!

Chapter

6

SECRETS TO SURVIVAL

Hopefully, you've been given a clear illustration of the extensive role leaders play in shaping the everyday working lives of the people around them. Their responsibilities go far beyond what is legally required by the government, and more is needed to achieve long-term goals then merely providing water, restrooms and scheduled breaks. It's not enough anymore to learn how to speak to people long enough to tell them what to do. True leaders must appeal to the intellect within each individual.

We've all dreamt of the perfect job where we receive a competitive salary that far exceeds the standard of living, benefits that value a family lifestyle (even if you don't have one), and surprise bonuses that have us constantly planning our next big vacation. Our ideology has colleagues respecting one another through open communication, teamwork and group learning. We have a boss who recognizes our abilities, assigns tasks that let us prove what we know and provides plenty of opportunities to learn from experts in our field. This job challenges us, makes us happy and allows us to confidentially proclaim, "I'm doing what I love! I'm exactly where I want to be."

How many people do you know who have that kind of picturesque job at this very moment? I'm guessing not too many. Looking around it seems that most people are too busy trying to survive than focusing on anything else. The poor quality of their work can be a reflection of that mental state, but leaving a job in search of something more catered to your needs is always easier said than done. So, people have a tendency to stay where they are, not because they like working in a toxic environment but because dreaming of a new life is much easier than actively moving towards one. Our hellish present is comfortably familiar while the potentially bright, unknown future can be frightening.

It's true that not everyone has the luxury to simply walk away. Many have families to support, more than one mouth to feed, perhaps daycare and education costs also. Most have a chunk of debt that refuses to shrink thanks to those high interest rates. And, with all our social responsibilities, the list of "necessary" purchases doesn't seem to be getting any shorter either—mortgage, cars, insurance, clothes, electronics, etc. So, perhaps you're feeling stuck at your current job like so many others around you. Until all your *Safety* needs are met, taking risks in pursuit of higher, intellectual goals (*Self-actualization*) isn't a luxury many of us can afford.

If you feel it's too risky to begin pursuing a journey further up the pyramid, it may help to better understand how to equip yourself for the daily struggle you're currently in. No one wants to babysit children without some diapers on hand, and people are more likely to go out in the midsummer sun if they know sunscreen and shade are readily available. Just the same, no one would go into battle without first gathering all the proper ammunition. Life is a whole lot easier when you've been prepped accordingly, even when it comes to walking through those office doors like clockwork almost every single day.

If you're in the unfortunate position of being surrounded by unwelcomed chaos in your everyday work life, then you may appreciate the survival topics found within the next few pages.

Can Bullshit Survive?
Oui, Si, 是, Ja, Sim, Da

Can bacteria grow on a toilet seat? Absolutely. But, as any high school biology class will teach us, there's less bacteria on a bathroom toilet then there is on a doorknob. After all, people wash their hands more often after using the toilet than they do after opening or closing a door. Disgusting, I know. That's also the main problem. While we're frantically disinfecting the toilet seats, the floors and the sinks, we're failing to address the real issue of where the bacteria originates, leaving it to spread all around.

Can bullshit survive? The disheartening answer will always be yes because we haven't gone to the core of the issue and cleansed our minds of the superficial sense of control that we get wrapped up in. Mediocre businesses will continue to survive and here are a few reasons why.

Good (Naïve) Employees

Some people will always think the best of others despite there being a disturbing amount of evidence to the contrary. There's a beautiful quality in maintaining that kind of mindset about others, but where do you draw the line when you are adversely affected. This reminds me of the classic fable of *The Scorpion and the Frog*. No matter how many times the scorpion boss wrongfully stings them, some employees will continue believing the broken record of fairytale phrases—"You're an essential part of our team," or, "Your hard work is going to pay off," or, "Everyone will get raises when things get better."

Good ol' Arthur didn't need this job but gave his word that he'd stay until the owners found more help. The only problem is that the owners weren't even looking. They jerked him around for not one month, not six months but over 24 months! His moral code was admirable but is it wise to keep promises with a scorpion whose innate response is to sting? Depending on which side of the spiritual spectrum you stand on, the answer may vary.

Giving leaders the benefit of the doubt is one thing but allowing them to walk all over you is another. Why is it that this type of employee still exists? This leads us to our next reason poorly managed businesses continue to survive.

Believable Lies

The pure of heart can't imagine a world where people can smile and lie to you at the same time. Even if that kind of innocence begins to see the light, it takes a large amount of energy to begin righteous confrontations, mental and physical energy they may not have anymore.

As my boss, Karen, proved daily, it's just easier for some leaders to believe the lies. But after that, more lies are then needed to cover up the compounding problems negatively reinforced by her choice to simply ignoring issues rather than solving them. The number of lies grew so quickly that it was inevitably difficult, or more accurately impossible, to keep track. But the rule of thumb was if something bad happened, it wasn't their fault. The boss could do no wrong. End of story. Facing the unfortunate truth of how a successful business begins to deteriorate is the first step to take accountability. But it's much easier to ignore problems then admit personal responsibility for failure. Perhaps, the problems will just go away on their own.

Scared Senseless

These people are constantly thinking about everything they have to lose and holding on to what little they do have for dear life. This is easy to sympathize with. Risk is something we become averse to when there's the potential to lose something of value like company benefits or consistent paychecks. Debt collection agencies are not in the business of providing life preservers. So, once again, jumping ship is a questionable option for many if not most people.

However, these prized possessions may not be the best floatation device. We often forget to imagine what will happen to us if we DON'T let go. What is the opportunity cost of staying at this job? What will I lose by staying where I am? If you've written "sacrifice happiness" anywhere on your list, it's time to begin developing an exit strategy and looking for other opportunities. Change can be terrifying. Sticking up for yourself can be, too. These are core reasons scaring people into staying exactly where they are with what little they still have works so well.

Soap Opera Decision-Making

These dramatic individuals are those who continually make the worst decisions possible. Within every scenario we're a part of, there's always a list of good and bad responses we can make. Everyone has a good angel and a bad angel on either shoulder. Each situation has multiple response options but these soap opera decision-makers hardly ever take the time needed to cultivate more than one possibility. They don't just choose from the bad list, they immediately jump to the top and choose the worst possible option. "No," they say to themselves, "I don't only want to leave all the lights on in my home when I leave. I'll also leave the fireplace on, too!" Another dramatic thought might be, "Why would I steal candy from the store when I could steal it from a baby?" Or, in the case of Karen and Herb, "Why would we garnish our wages in rough times when we could easily garnish our employee's wages?" If they saw a house on fire, they would choose to throw gasoline on top of it rather than water. And if it were thunder and lightning outside, they would raise a metal chalice in toasting to Mother Nature.

These types of decision-makers wouldn't stop their destructive pattern if you tied them to a stop sign and beat them senselessly. There's no debate on whether the majority of people will typically choose an easier decision over a hard one, and the bad list of responses are full of easy choices compared to the good list. However, these quick and simple choices are made for short-term relief to long-term problems. It's by far the road most traveled. Robert Frost would have a field day.

Jerk Alert
Secrets to Failure

Let's first identify if your boss is actually a jerk or if you're perpetually having bad days for other reasons. For assistance, there are some of the most alarmingly obvious triggers your boss is a jerk provided on the next page. All these behaviors are a part of their preferred, ego-based leadership style. They will do anything to feel they have complete control over their surroundings and, more importantly, over their subordinates. The majority of their days are spent in isolation or taunting the people around them. The only reason they choose to have human interaction is so they can make their power plays of the day. No response is needed on your end because this type of leader has already enjoyed a few moments at your expense and is already headed back to their office throne.

Does your boss or supervisor do any of the following? Check out these classic warning signs.

JERK ALERT!

- JOKES at your expense
- EXPECTS credit for your work
- RIDICULES you publically
- KILLS your opportunities for growth
- ADVANCES inappropriately
- LISTENS never, interrupts always
- EVADES accountability
- REJECTS the validity of your contributions
- THREATENS you as a form of motivation

J – <u>JOKES</u> at your expense – Your boss definitely thinks they're the funniest person in the office. This is evidenced by the fact that they're always the only one laughing (with the exception of a few of those obsequious bystanders). The jokes are typically direct, personal attacks and have little to do with work-related topics. The victim will typically pretend to let it go while harboring resentful feelings.

E – <u>EXPECTS</u> credit for your work – Your superior doesn't feel the need to justify this because he's paying you. Everything you accomplish belongs to him and the company. He's not big on praise, so you may not ever know your contributions are valuable until you overhear your boss trying to impress his own superiors or outsiders by claiming the work as his own. He'll use all "I" and "me" terminology rather than "we" or "us." You'll hear, "I developed a new strategy to generate more revenue," rather than, "I developed a new strategy based on the data my team collected." Don't expect any credit unless, of course, you make a mistake.

R – <u>RIDICULES</u> you publically – This is similar to joking around except ridiculing will be more work focused. Insulting your intelligence in front of your colleagues is a huge bonus for your boss too because it asserts his reign over his kingdom rather than over just one subject. You are his poster child of a bad example and he won't fail to remind everyone of your faults, even if he has to make them up.

K – <u>KILLS</u> your opportunities for advancement – Learning is one of the most important aspects of every job. But, if your boss is a jerk, don't expect any chances for growth. Suppressing you is one definite way to maintain a clear divide in authority. This behavior is often incognito within the rhetorical question, "Why would I support your education when you would just end up leaving the company?" With a strategically placed glass ceiling, you can never become a threat to his position or disrupt his emotional need for supremacy. Holding you back allows him to maintain a Catch-22 scenario where he can continue making outrageous demands you can never hope to satisfy. Knowledge is power and you're not allowed to have any.

A – <u>ADVANCES</u> inappropriately – Your jerky boss successfully crosses almost every emotional boundary, so invading your physical space should come as no surprise.

Not everyone is comfortable using their bodies to interact with others (mostly because one touch has convinced our sue-happy culture to speed-dial our lawyer), but those who do with negative, manipulative intensions have a personal vendetta. Others may use their hands to touch, arms to hug or body to slam. It just depends on the personal comfort level of your very own boss-jerk. However, advanced manipulators don't have to touch you at all to invade your personal space. Some are comfortable enough with confrontation to step inches from your face, pushing intentional threats of unwelcomed physical interactions.

L – <u>LISTENS</u> never, interrupts always – It can be difficult communicating a full thought because there's usually only one keynote speaker for every conversation. And, since your boss loves the sound of their own voice, the obvious goes without saying. Interrupting your verbal contributions and chopping the flow and rhythm of your thought process is just another way to maintain submission. You feel invisible, worthless and stupid. You may even forget why you stepped into your boss's office in the first place, furthering their win.

E – <u>EVADES</u> accountability – You remember how your boss-jerk expects credit for all your work? With that same amount of enthusiasm, you can expect him to evade accountability, too. They might say, "That was your job, your responsibility. Not mine." That way, if you mess up, he gets to point fingers, feeding you to the wolves rather than standing behind the work his team was delegated.

However, if you're successful, he's successful and your work is no longer your own.

R - <u>REJECTS</u> the validity of your contributions - You're damn good at your job. You know the ins-and-outs of your department and going above and beyond is a comfortable requirement you often do without being asked. Your colleagues in the office appreciate working along side you and those clients you work with on the outside value your professionalism and insight. Despite all this, there's one person who won't acknowledge your efforts—your boss. Even if you're bold enough to openly address your accomplishments, expect to be completely shutdown.

T - <u>THREATENS</u> you as a form of motivation - Your boss wants something from you but you show resistance. Since these jerks rarely practice having a true discussion where there's an exchange of ideas from more than one participant, the only option they give themselves (showing an enormous lack of creativity if you ask me) is to threaten you. "If you don't put in an effort, we may have to cut back people's hours at work."

Not all of these poor management traits need to be checked off in order to brand your boss as a jerk. Just like you, their skills may excel in one area over another. Perhaps they prefer lashing out verbally more than making inappropriate physical advances. Some may be more skilled at manipulating situations to amplify their success rather than making direct threats towards another person.

This type of toxic behavior is meant to belittle subordinates while uplifting themselves. Because the person causing the chaos can never find a source of personal security or real focus, these behaviors don't stop. Their number one daily focus is himself or herself. When they feel threatened, you can expect childlike behaviors to surface like finger-pointing, avoiding eye contact and even name-calling.

Offending or making your boss look like an idiot is an awfully tempting form of retaliation but not the best idea. I did this once. Being female, the youngest person in the office and dressing nicer than everyone else wished to, Herb tried using me as his personal secretary. He wanted me to print documents for him, direct his personal calls, screen his visitors, everything expect sharpening his pencils. Refusing to let him undervalue my capabilities and current responsibilities by replacing them with fluff, I said, "I'm sure *you're* capable of doing that." Such a simple phrase doesn't sound like a big deal but when it's publicly directed to the president of your company who has more insecurities than a pimply, high school freshman, there's going to be a backlash.

SECRETS TO GET PEOPLE TO HATE YOU

Practice all the secrets to failure found above.

Tips for Survival
Lithium

You're blamed for their mistakes, you're publically ridiculed on a daily basis and no one acknowledges your contributions, and yet, you still can't just walk away. If you don't have the ability to leave your job at this very moment, I wouldn't feel right about sending you back in without some extra ammunition. So, before you start tossing laxatives into your boss's coffee or throwing darts at their picture (although, temporarily stress relieving), you may want to consider a few tactics that have more of a long-term focus. If your attempts to have a civilized conversation with your boss fail worse than a P90X workout attempt, ask yourself, "Do I need a whole suit of battle armor for this fight or just a sling?" Here are ten tips to help you survive working for a boss from hell.

Tip #1: Make Your Boss Look Good

Give them what they want. This is the same advice I regularly give to students. Getting the best grades in school is not necessarily knowing all the right answers, it's about giving your professors what they want, not what you want to give them. It doesn't matter how right you are. If the professor does not agree, your grade will suffer.

The same is true for the working world as it is for the scholastic world. Those that get ahead are the ones who make their boss look good and give them exactly what they've asked for. The most frustrating part is that it doesn't even matter if you're smarter than the head honcho. They probably won't ever admit it, but your boss is needy. He appreciates the power to control. Cater to his professional and personal needs but on your own terms. There's no need to get your nose dirty.

Tip #2: Document, Document, Document

I can't stress this enough. In the legalistic world we live in today, your word is unfortunately not good enough. It should be in an idealistic, utopian-filled community of good people. But, alas, there is no better protection than consistent and thorough documentation. The rookie mistake is to only document the negative interactions between coworkers. The boss angrily slammed a large binder down right beside my colleague's face or the manager yelled profanity at his team. (Yes. I've personally witnessed these happening.) He said/she said scenarios are a good start but don't stop there. Other important aspects of your job to document include:

- Work – new documents created, connections made, projects assigned/completed, milestones achieved
- Attendance – days, hours
- Formal Requests – time off, promotion applications, raise requests
- Meetings – date, time, topics
- Questionable Behavior – includes all work colleagues (not just those above you in rank), how you coped with the situation, final resolve

Make sure the social laws of documentation are also respected. When you make important, professional comments or requests via email (a great choice because it's officially documented), make sure your leadership responds in the same fashion you originally started communicating in. One of Karen's favorite techniques to avoid a paper trail on sensitive issues was to respond to an employee's email in person. Or, to avoid a confrontation, she would send HR to respond on her behalf. Efficient, verbal communication is paramount to surviving any work environment, but no matter how good it is, don't let it replace written documentation. Not all verbal contracts are binding, but no judicial system can deny physical documents.

One exception to my earnest suggestion for documentation is that I choose not to document situations that I did not personally witness. However, if I spend large amounts of time consoling a fellow employee who is distraught over seeing gay porn on their boss's computer, I would definitely document that. A friend making general complaints of how mean the boss is, I leave that out.

Tip #3: Create a Support System

Teaming up with others helps remind us of the value we possess and validates our accomplishments. Remember, there's strength in numbers, and its much harder to fight large battles on our own.

Coworkers – Branch out and get to know more than just your immediate colleagues. Befriend people above and below your position and in different departments as well. No matter how different everyone's job may be, nothing brings people together better than a common enemy.

Friends/family – Venting is a great way to relieve stress and avoid the negative repercussions of bottling up your emotions. However, I'll caution you against using this group for daily therapy. There's a big difference between this and the occasional gripe-fest. These people in your personal life did not necessarily choose the career of a professional counselor, but they are great for filling your days with non-work related activities when your spirits need a friendly boost.

Counselor – Confiding in an objective professional can provide more than one helpful prospective that you didn't have before, and there are few things more valuable than having the opportunity to see from someone else's viewpoint. A good counselor will help you establish personal goals and assist you in tackling difficult decisions.

Lawyer – Befriending a lawyer is easier than it sounds. If you don't already have one amongst your circle of friends, you can easily call around to ask for a (free) consultation. These advisors can provide crucial information on how to protect yourself so that legal action can be avoided. However, if legal action is required, it bodes well for you that these professionals love nothing more than taking down an opponent. Many people avoid taking legal action because they view it as more drama their life could do without. Although, it's good to remember that there's no harm in educating yourself by listening to the experts. You don't have to do anything. In fact, you shouldn't until you have all the facts anyway.

Internet – If you're looking for people who you know can relate with a toxic working environment, the web has several options. There are articles, blogs, group chats and webinars all dedicated to those who have had terrible experiences in the workplace. (Plug: Visit a website I cofounded called OfficeFromHell.com for ridiculously funny and horrifically true stories about the worst leaders on the planet. You can also share your personal stories and find others who can relate.)

Tip #4: Alter Your Perspective

This is definitely a game-changer worth trying. Those who wake up hating work will inevitably hate work when they get there. Happiness is a choice and we must constantly remind ourselves to put the positives in the forefront of our thoughts rather than the negative. Just like every other worthwhile task, changing the way we think can take some practice. Instead of focusing on hating your boss, try also feeling bad for them because they're clearly depressed, lonely and/or have low self-esteem.

You can also identify some other positive attributes of your work environment. Perhaps you're able to learn a great deal while other jobs don't have those same opportunities. Maybe you work with friends or are making new ones. I don't mean to sound like I'm writing an ad for PBS Kids, but positive thoughts have been proven to help shift your mental focus throughout the day. You should give it a fair try.

Tip #5: Become Self-Seeking

Take a moment to think about everything your job has to offer. Work can be so much more than just a paycheck if you want it to be. My colleague Kevin had so much downtime at the office that he'd spend half the day performing tasks for a completely different job he held that management knew nothing about. I could relate with his value of time. Back in college, I preferred working desk jobs, like a receptionist, because I could do my homework during the moments when I wasn't helping people. Now, what extra perks does your job have available?

Overtime – Pick-up some extra work shifts to buffer your bank account.

Education – Take advantage of learning opportunities that can help make your resume more attractive to future employers. Your work doesn't pay for classes? That's ok. Have a colleague teach you a new computer program or ask to sit in on conference calls/meetings to broaden your understanding of the industry you're in.

Networking – Maintain relationships with everyone your current job has brought you into contact with both inside the office and outside. Collect contact information and perhaps even connect with them on professional, social media sites like LinkedIn.

Tip #6: Daydream

There's nothing wrong with a healthy distraction but keep it in moderation (after all, we are supposed to be working). Perhaps you love thinking about where you'll fly to on your next exotic vacation or planning a party to spend time with friends. Maybe your daytime fantasies have you becoming the next member of the *Avengers*. Yes, I'm sharing personal daydreams now. Getting lost in my thoughts, I was spontaneous, clever and strategically organized in my fight against the bad guys. I would have made MacGyver proud.

With Karen breathing fire under everyone's desk chair, my favorite daydream of all was imagining my escape (exit strategy). Because I followed Tip #5, my daydream became rather elaborate and detail oriented. Planning ten steps ahead helped me establish goals dictating how much time I would remain at the office from hell, how much of a financial cushion I could acquire before leaving and increase the number of friendships that could form out of mere acquaintances.

Tip #7: Seek Balance

Becoming well-rounded by balancing our needs is essential to making life easier on ourselves. However, nothing will help if you've neglected to build a healthy routine on solid ground. All legs get shake on a rocky foundation, so make sure to meet your immediate, physical needs at the start and end of every day in order to make productive efforts upward. Eat healthy, exercise and get plenty of rest. This always seems to be easier said than done, but maintaining your physical health will become one of the biggest supporters of your mental health by decreasing your susceptibility to anxiety, stress and eventual illness.

Exercise – This means both physically and mentally. Go to the gym or for a long walk outdoors. Keep that heart pumping so it doesn't stop. Work out your mind by reading or playing games, too. Stay engaged by doing activities that are out of the ordinary for you or have been on your bucket list for years. Perhaps you can even combine the physical and mental workouts! Meditation yoga anyone?

Sleep – Don't underestimate the power of some quality shut-eye. I'm personally a big fan of a full eight hours. Keep me up into the wee hours of the morning and I'll just start talking gibberish. I'll be so tired that you could probably ask me any outlandish question and I'd answer it. It works better than an alcohol-based truth serum for me. But, be warned, I'm worthless with less than six hours of sleep.

Tip #8: Sense of Humor

Have one. Laughing is good for every part of your body including the brain. Letting some personal quarrels go can be good, too. Take your work environment as it is and remember a groundbreaking factoid—people can be ridiculous. So, laugh and laugh often.

Tip #9: People 101

If you want to make one of the smartest moves of your life, study personality types to improve your human interaction skills. You're already an expert in your industry, so now it's time to educate yourself on the people within that industry. You may already get along with people in general but attempting to fully understand the thought process of those you work with can mend a lot of gaps in the day-to-day assignments and make communication that much easier for everyone involved. Learning about the similarities and differences of people is essential if you want to be successful. Get to know your colleagues by listening and understanding their approach to work and their approach to life.

The most common excuse I hear regarding the people aspect of our work life is, "Why bother? I'm not here to make friends. I'm here to work." Just because we were born human doesn't automatically make us good at being one or an expert on understanding them. Like it or not, you can't succeed without the help of others. If we ignore this, we're no better than the infamously selfish Karen and Herb.

Another perfect example of this ignorance can be found in the one trash-TV show I allow myself to get sucked into—The Bachelor. (Don't worry, I judge me, too.) Every season, I notice at least one male or female amongst the pack that is hated by all others. In a house full of heightened expectations, this person has the same intensions as everyone else (to become the chosen one by the bachelor/bachelorette) but go about it in a different, toxic way. This self-proclaimed outcast chooses to be mean, nasty, conniving and blatantly rude to everyone around them. When confronted about their poor behavior, they say those famously evasive words, "I'm not here to make friends." The end result is always the same. This type of person never marries the bachelor/bachelorette and never wins.

Tip #10: Run!

Sometimes walking away is the healthiest and most professional thing you can do. A potential roadblock to this is when people feel the need to make their peace or get closure with the issues at hand. Much of the time, however, there's no point. You won't get any satisfaction out of confronting crazy more than you already have, and a bullet in your back isn't exactly the parting gift you'll want to take with you.

Avoid Hellish Leaders
Victory Is Yours

If you have plans to get a new job anytime in the future, here are a few tips on how to avoid working in a toxic environment created by a hellish boss. Use these tips to improve your visibility of employee smoke signals and employer red flags so you don't end up raising one yourself. Below are a few tasks you should consider doing.

Tip #1: Do Your Research

Don't underestimate the power of prep work. Dedicate some time researching a potential employer before attending an interview. Look for customer reviews (both pros and cons), find mission statements, press releases, even do a soft background check on company management to get a better understanding of their experience. Your visit will not only be more relaxing because of your preparedness, but you'll have the power to assess your interviewer properly. That's right! The interview goes both ways.

Tip #2: Ask Questions

I've compiled a list of my top five, favorite questions to ask an interviewer. All of them help to assess whether your future boss has a firm grasp on the current situation and knows how to clearly communicate them to others. If they don't know how, move on!

> 1) *"What are the company's current goals and how are you wanting this position to contribute?"*

What this question tells you: This gives you a better picture of how realistic the company is and how "big picture" their mindset can be.

What this question tells the interviewer: You are a goal-oriented person who values clear communication.

> 2) *"What are some of the reasons the last (job title) is no longer in this position?"*

If your interviewer struggles to give a direct answer, take note. This may have to do with confidentiality or even personal pride. You can ease the tension by following up with a few less invasive questions they can choose from such as, "Were there performance areas they openly struggled with?" or, "Did they get promoted within the company?"

What this question tells you: What the interviewer says and doesn't say are both very important. Whether they open up about the last person's abilities or withhold information, both responses have the potential to provide you ample knowledge about your potential employer and the workload they'll expect you to carry.

What this question tells the interviewer: You are making a conscious effort to determine whether or not you are a good fit within the company and if your efforts will be valued.

3) "What has the culture been like since you've been with the company?

Personal questions create a relaxed, more conversational environment that allows the interviewer a chance to chat about themselves, and listening to them is a type of compliment. Make sure to focus on what they're saying.

What this question tells you: This provides a good idea of how much your interviewer enjoys his job and the people he works with.

What this question tells the interviewer: You value the personal opinions and wisdom of the individual in front of you.

4) "Are there opportunities provided for educational growth and learning?"

Examples may include attending conferences, seminars, paid classes within your field and several other options.

What this question tells you: This gives you a glimpse of their value system. Those who don't invest in continued growth and education often fail to invest in their employees in other ways as well.

What this question tells the interviewer: You're a knowledgeable asset and you wish to continue using that knowledge to benefit the industry you're in.

5) "Were there any areas in my resume that you found valuable or sections you felt were unclear?"

This provides you with one last chance to showcase your skills. Always end on a high note.

What this question tells you: This may highlight potential errors you've made in your resume. If a section of this document confused them or was not thorough enough for one person, there's a good chance this would be the case for others as well.

What this question tells the interviewer: You appreciate the thoughts of others and can accept constructive criticism.

If all your pre-planned questions were already answered during the interview, don't panic. I encourage you to call it like it is. Mention the questions you would have asked and communicate what answers were provided. This shows your ability to listen and regurgitate information accurately.

Tip #3: Assess Your Interviewer

Your interviewer is not the only one trying to see if you would make a good fit within their company. You should also be assessing the business to see if it's a good fit for you, too. If an interviewer talks extensively more than an interviewee does, the interviewer is either full of themselves, nervous or has already decided whom they're going to hire for the position in question. Also, be wary of interviewers who seem overly eager to get you on board. It's easy to get caught up in the niceties and forget to elaborate on important issues. Stay focused so you can get a clear picture of the environment you're about to step into.

Tip #4: Know Your Worth

If they try to lowball you regarding pay or benefits, you have every right to negotiate. If they don't or don't know how, it's probably best to walk away. After all, you get what you pay for, and if leaders aren't willing to pay for you, their priorities may be shifted in the wrong direction. Superficial or not, financial compensation can be a great indicator of how much respect you have within a company.

Tip #5: Check Your Moral Compass

Some call befriending your hellish boss a necessary evil. Despite all the good that can come from this, developing a relationship with your superiors also means you may have more opportunities to slay the colleagues closest to you. You'll be able to jump ahead of them at every turn, amplifying your own accomplishments while downplaying theirs. How far are you willing to go at the expense of the other people on your team?

Final Thoughts
Chapter 6

Many of us are in a position where we are simultaneously leading others while being led ourselves. We are both a superior and a subordinate, a leader and a follower, a captain and a crewmember. That means we have personal experience on both sides of the spectrum that can help us be sympathetic to and better understand the personal needs within both worlds. (Hint: Maslow's pyramid doesn't change, so the core needs remain the same no matter what position you hold at work.)

It doesn't matter if you work for a large, *Fortune 500* company in the city or a small brick and mortar in a country town, teams of people help make that entity a success. Whether you're teaching in a school, accounting for a nonprofit organization, taking shifts at a community hospital or selling hand-crafted items from the comfort of your own home, you'll find yourself in a leadership position at one point or another.

Maslow did the working world a favor when he stacked our needs in an order that makes sense because people are, without a doubt, the most important variable in all of business. Even as the development of robotics and automated machines continue to advance, the attempt to cut costs by eliminating the need for human labor still does not wipe out the need for human maintenance. So, unless Steven Spielberg's robots take over as superior beings, the human element in our working lives will always be stable and ultimately necessary. No matter what industry you've chosen to work in, you are relevant and your contributions are important.

A Team Member Read

Is there a way to speed up the process to enjoying the happiness and satisfaction found within *Self-actualization*? Yes! There is! As previously mentioned, self-reflection is the best way to *Self-actualization*. People who are aware of their own needs, desires and abilities are typically happier than most because they can pinpoint areas of focus that motivate their progress forward. In fact, climbing up the hierarchy is primarily an individual responsibility. The leaders in your working world are a secondary support and a strong one at that.

How can you maintain a healthy level of self-awareness? Make sure to check in with yourself the same way you would a close friend or family member and ask, "How am I doing?" If you struggle to give a firm answer, take a look at the pyramid below and pick a weather forecast that closely resembles your current state. That way you'll have a better idea of where you are, where you can go from that point and how you can get there.

Not all businesses will cater to your specific needs, which is why your selection of an employer is so important. Some entities are not built around maintaining high-income employees. So, if you work at a fast food restaurant, don't expect management to restructure their bulletproof franchise system to accommodate your need for more money. If you're a parking meter attendant with a high need for socialization, I wouldn't blame your supervisor for a lack of companionship. We must take some responsibility from the very beginning to know what our needs are before we start blaming others for not meeting them. We also have more control over our working environments than we are often led to believe.

No matter what your job is or the industry you work in, it's employees like you who have the ability to push innovative ideas into the world. People are behind the development of sophisticated societies, the reason grand structures are built and why the tech industry will continue its boom. They are the dedicated workers who wake a business up in the morning and sweep the floors before locking up at night.

Question: Have you ever watched a young person get arrested? If so, did you feel bad for them? Did you wonder what pushed them to the point of criminal behavior? Was it something in their past? Perhaps they grew up with dispassionate parents who told them they were worthless, friends who distrusted them and teachers who looked down on them. You could imagine the destruction of their potential years before the tipping point ever reared its ugly head. If only they have been given a chance. If only someone had provided them an environment to thrive in, an environment to explore their own value. That's exactly my train of thought when I watch teams of people trying to function in a thoughtless work environment with incompetent leadership.

Those that are not overseen by supportive leadership are stuck with gorilla-sized distractions that inhibit their ability to advance in the *Hierarchy of Needs*. So, I encourage you to make a conscience choice to live a working life free of toxicity.

A Leadership Read

There's a good chance that one day you'll be promoted to a position where you will lead others if you haven't been so already. In preparation, you can read thousands of books about the true meaning of management but a snapshot definition of a great leader would be their ability to intuitively recognize the potential of others, provide a safe environment to amplify those skills and then direct that self-motivated energy towards a productive purpose.

Can't or won't? Which is worse? Failing in your ventures because you didn't have the necessary resources for business or failing because you chose not to utilize the resources you did have? You can't properly delegate responsibilities to other professionals or you *won't* delegate to them? You can't hear the needs of your team or you *won't* hear them?

They say the only thing worse than trying and failing is not trying at all. Well, if you have assembled an experienced and capable team but don't allow them to do the jobs for which they've been hired, you have not tried. The demise of your enterprise was as inevitable as if you never had those human resources at all. Hiring a capable staff is not trying. Getting out of their way so they can get some work done, however, is.

Companies are typically painted in society as inhuman entities (especially the large corporations), void of all worthy, human characteristics. Although, I appreciate finding successful businesses to be quite the opposite. Just as people can educate themselves and become enlightened in their fields of study, so too can a business grow intelligently by addressing the needs of it's components— the individuals that make up their team. A business is so much more than an inanimate object. To the contrary, a business is the sum of its human qualities.

What keeps people motivated to work for another person or, more specifically, for you? This question begs Maslow to remind us of the kind of working world we could live in if leaders knew how to tap into the true strength of their human resources. How would the office environment change if everyone enjoyed coming into work everyday? And, by recourse, how much happier would our customers be if they saw how much employees appreciated their responsibilities?

All the major decisions made regarding the development of a company's culture and utilization of human resources begin at the top where influential managers can be found. So, that's exactly where the changes need to begin. You must first focus on becoming an environment leader internally if you have any hopes of dominating externally as an industry leader.

In the meantime, while management teams continue seeking out leadership advice from the Grim Reaper in the corner office, let's focus on what it takes for guaranteed failure. Don't worry. It's easy. Anyone can stab themselves in the leg!

The best news of all is that if you want to be the one who presses that irresistible red button and begin the self-destruct timer for the business you work for, you don't have to be the owner. You can easily be in any leadership position and follow these simple steps towards an inevitable downfall.

Take note of these five classic leadership fails that demolish growth and sustainability. 1) Suppress the dreams your employees or team may have of influencing others by reinforcing a glass ceiling at every opportunity within *Self-actualization*. (2 Ignore important delegation responsibilities by assigning tasks not aligned with your team's individual skillset within the *Esteem* stage. 3) Alienate their need to belong in the environment of like-minded individuals by demeaning their efforts within the *Social* stage. 4) Demolish their sense of security by making promises you can't or won't keep within the *Safety* stage. And last but certainly not least, 5) push them down further still by ignoring their basic needs as fellow human beings within the *Physiological* stage.

If you lose your way on your quest for failure, just remember that you're pushing your human resources down rather than lifting them up because…

YOU'RE NOT DOING IT RIGHT UNLESS YOU'RE DOING IT WRONG!

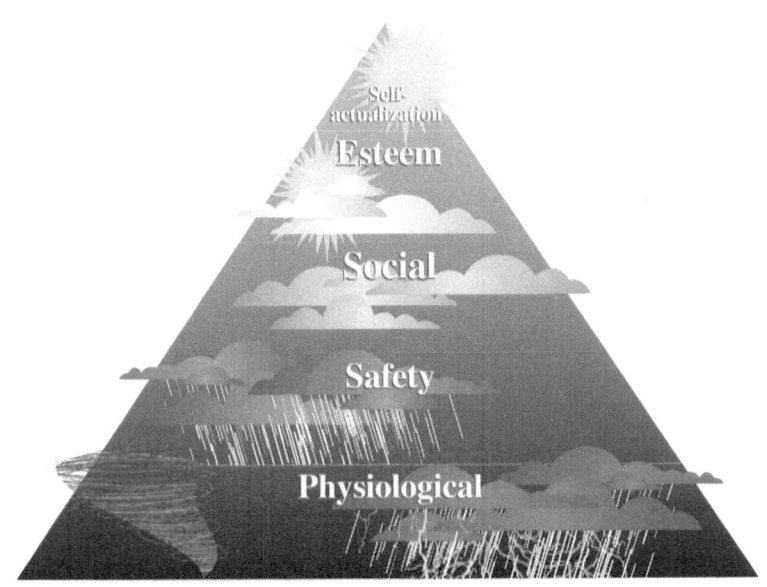

Epilogue

Since the completion of this unconventional leadership book, a chain of events have unfolded that provide the cherry on top of this destructive sundae. It's easy to end a work story with a company lying in rubble. It's concrete enough that you, the reader, can feel somewhat of a resolution upon closing the book. But, I'll do you one better.

Would you like to know what happened to Karen and Herb? Last we hear from them, they're quietly slipping out of the picture altogether, golden parachute in tow, when the company changes hands. The company and its employed inhabitants became someone else's problem because they successfully washed their hands clean(ish).

A few months down the road, however, the same investment firm who had saved their collective ass from personal, financial ruin did a complete 180 turnaround. Several weeks of crunching real numbers indicated that everything they had been warned about was true. Karen and Herb had lied about absolutely everything—the client retention, the available clinician support and how many people used their services among other things. The numbers were clearly illuminating the current position of the new owners and how they had voluntarily boarded a sinking ship. But, not for long.

An email was forwarded by the new owners to everyone connected with the company, both past and present, that highlighted the false information the business acquisition was based on and demanded that the original owners, along with their board of directors, reinstate themselves immediately because these new leaders weren't going to stick around anymore to clean up someone else's mess.

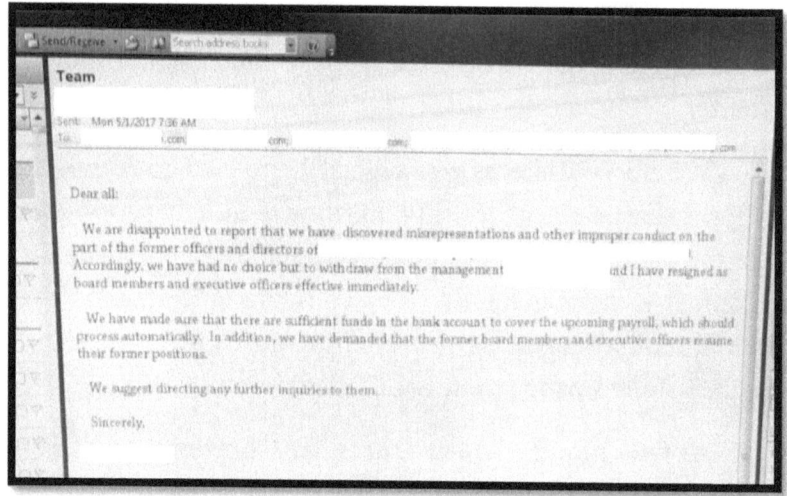

For an easier read, the above (redacted) email says the following:

> "Dear all: We are disappointed to report that we have discovered misrepresentations and other improper conduct on the part of the former officers and directors of [XXX]. Accordingly, we have had no choice but to withdraw from the management of [XXX]. [XXX] and I have resigned as board members and executive officers effective immediately. We have made sure that there are sufficient funds in the bank account to cover the

upcoming payroll, which should process automatically. In addition, we have demanded that the former board members and executive officers resume their former positions. We suggest directing any further inquiries to them. Sincerely, [XXX]."

Through all their struggles to maintain focus on their own selfish endeavors, Karen and Herb are now in the middle of a lawsuit that entangles their personal property. It's two bobbleheads up against an investment firm that has substantial resources and can make good on their threats. Currently, word has it that Karen and Herb are avoiding a subpoena by ignoring every person who comes to the front door of their home.

That's not the only thing they'll have to avoid. The investment firm also sent that "peace out" email to all the client company's that would potentially be affected including banks, state universities, hospitals, retail businesses and several others. Karen and Herb's personal contact information was also provided for the convenience of all.

It's true what they say about vindication. It feels great.

About the Author

J. D. Allen is a marketing consultant and entrepreneur who specializes in helping businesses reach their target markets. Allen has grandeur thoughts of becoming one of the most well-respected minds within the world of organizational psychology but is far too busy proving generational research correct by working less and playing more.

To stay in touch and receive free updates and exclusive offers, join the newsletters found on these sites below:

♦

An Underground Library for the Curious Mind

Book: www.GoldenArrowPublishing.com

Highlighting Creative Businesses That Add Value To Our Lives

Blog: www.JentleBiz.com

www.ingramcontent.com/pod-product-compliance
Lightning Source LLC
Chambersburg PA
CBHW020654220526
45464CB00001B/435